AS IT WAS
IN THE BEGINNING

VOLUME ONE

EWURAMMA

Our Paraclete

Certificate of Marriage

This certifies that

ADAM & **EVE**

Were united in Marriage

On the **SIXTH** Day of **CREATION** the year **BEGINNING**

Witnessed by **JESUS CHRIST** & **HOLY SPIRIT**

Celebrated by **GOD THE FATHER**

AS IT WAS IN THE BEGINNING

Copyright © 2023 by Ewuramma
All rights reserved.

ISBN: 978-1-524763-1-3

E-Book ISBN: 978-1-524763-1-5

Copyright © 2023 Our Paraclete. All rights reserved.

Published by: Our Paraclete, an imprint of Our Paraclete Publishers.

All rights reserved. No part of this book may be reproduced or transmitted in any form or by any means, electronic or mechanical, including photocopying, recording, or by any information storage and retrieval system, without permission in writing from the publisher.

Unless otherwise indicated, all Scriptures are taken from the Holy Bible, Amplified Bible, Classic Edition®, AMPC®. Copyright © 1962, 1964, 1965, 1987 by Biblica, Inc.™, used by permission of Zondervan. All rights reserved worldwide. www.zondervan.com. The "NIV" and "New International Version" are trademarks registered in the United States Patent and Trademark Office by Biblica, Inc.

Contact Author on:

ourparacletefoundation.inc@gmail.com

Design & Print by:

Indes Procom Ltd.
www.indesprocom.com

Cover Credit:

Richard Opoku Agyeman
Director, Acute Formula

CONTENTS OF VOL. I

Dedication	*vi*
Apologia	*ix*
Foreword	*xiii*
Endorsements	*xviii*

CHAPTER 01
The Origin of The Human Race — *01*

CHAPTER 02
The Church of God — *19*

CHAPTER 03
The Society — *24*

CHAPTER 04
Family Responsibility — *43*

CHAPTER 05
The Church Is A Mother — *58*

CHAPTER 06
The Two Inevitable Institutions — *100*

CHAPTER 07
The Private Conscience And Judgement — *110*

CHAPTER 08
Gender Relations — *120*

CHAPTER 09
The Mystery of Marriage — *158*

CHAPTER 10
The Eden's Garden — *206*

DEDICATION

I dedicate the book to the man who was my elder, father and friend,
Elder Thomas Godfrey Kofi Gyampoh

"In the year when king Uzziah died I saw also the Lord sitting upon a throne, high and lifted up, and his train filled the temple." Isaiah 6:1

Before anyone knew I could do anything in the house of God in the United States, you told me what I had not seen. In my girlhood, while I was yet a stripling, you persuaded me to be an adult Christian and play the woman for God of my fathers and mothers.

No one can ever overestimate the great privilege God has given me through your help and nurture in God. In my girlhood mind, I did not understand why you assigned me to lead worship every time the then national Head Apostle Alex Osei Bonsu and the then New York District pastor Overseer Andrew Kwabena Donkor visited our assembly (Queens). As it's typical of me, I approached you but asked a seemingly negative question. "Elder, why do you want to drive me away from the church?" You laughed and calmly said: "No, God has deposited something in you, and I want to help you."

You loved the Lord who has called you to Himself so very much; hence, you loved everyone and everything that promoted His course. We all were not able, as yet, to bear the full revelation of Providence when He permitted me to be taken away from you and Mama Vida's guardianship. But Our Lord Jesus possessed the wisdom to understand it all.

Satan did everything to have made me forget the God of my fathers. Everywhere around me, I saw sorrow and heartache. I had so much to tell you every time I saw you, but I became dumb for over a decade.

On that fateful day when you persuaded me to talk, you did something that is not often said about African men. You wept. Your tears were a very Instructive fact to me. It was full of consolation to tell me that someone cared about me. You are a man yet with a woman's heart. Anyone who knows can never doubt how strict and principled you were. Yet as a man, you lived, related, and cared as a Mother HEN covering everyone that crossed paths with you with your wings. Oh, how I wish you could hear me say that I will arise by the grace of God. I will become everything you saw God could make me become.

I am also sure God that I will not only be a specimen of a tried Christian but also of a specimen of a graced Christian. And God will surely be praised for every moment of my life. When you bowed your head to death, it, in fact, reminded a new me of the origin of my commission — Go ye, therefore, and teach all nations (Mark 16:15). Having life and motion, I will use my pain-turned-power with prudence and discretion. My biography will never end with the false triumph of the devil over me.

There is no word capable of conveying all that I mean to say. But I want to assure you that by the Word of our Lord Jesus and by His Spirit, I mean to win the victory. By the testimony of a weak and feeble me to the gospel of Jesus' grace, I mean to conquer the powers of darkness.

I thank you and Mama Vida and all the children for everything. May your gentle and selfless soul continue to rest in the bosom of our Lord and Savior, Jesus Christ.

— Ewuramma

Apologia

Most people I know, who marry, hope their relationship will be like Romeo and Juliet's if not the Titanic love story. And while many of them see their dreams come true, many other promising marriages struggle, and others, unfortunately, end in divorce.

What's the trick? Is it just that those who enjoy their marriages and stay married know better how to choose their life partners than those who do not? Of course, many reasons could be offered; at the very least, many justifications could be revised. My thoughts on the subject are as follows: A married relationship is the consequence of *faith* and *love*. Thus, it takes absolute faith and love for two finite people to entrust the rest of their lives and their children's to someone they cannot know who and what they will become in the next 10 seconds. Nevertheless, it is faith that motivates them to make such a courageous move. And whenever and wherever faith sets out to achieve something, she is joined by love.

Although many people believe that any man or any woman makes a good husband or a good wife, I respectfully disagree. A godly and loyal man or woman who seeks an everlasting relationship seeks a spouse who is like them in character and preference. A survey study of over 10,000 people looking for marriage partners discovered that kindness was "universally sought". While a man seeks a kindhearted wife, a woman seeks someone with a matching disposition. In a broad sense, a kindhearted person is a loyal person. They are selfless and have the grace and capacity to build friendships and empathy when it comes to parenting children.

Marriage is also a choice, and most people consider it to be an enlightening and happy experience. Regardless of how two people enter a marriage, whether, by choice or arrangement, it is not legitimate until there is a choice on both sides to make the marriage work. Couples who are compelled into marriages in cultures that still recognize arranged marriages do not abandon the marriage even if they are initially very dissatisfied. They do not end the relationship and move on with their lives. Instead, by sticking together, they make it work.

Choice of marriage and choice in the marriage must be mutual. It implies that both sides should have a blessed choice to make it a true marriage.

It is unhealthy when there is a stark contrast between a husband and a wife; when one is on the extreme left and the other on the far right. In such a home, no matter how much God may bless the family in all other respects, there will be a great miss in it. Like the eclipsed sun, that part of family life that should be all light will be left in thick darkness.

A very similar analogy is the American election of a president and vice president in 2020. It serves in both roles to the great benefit of depicting a home and how the human race began in the Garden of Eden. The then former Vice President Joseph Robinette Biden, the Democratic presidential nominee at the time, was like an eligible bachelor. President Joseph R. Biden, like Adam, required a helpmate to assist him in managing his household (America) and parenting his children (American citizens). Thus, he had absolute power over the significant person he chose to label "Vice President" in his cabinet. That is when faith emerges as an unavoidable virtue.

Apologia

In his very delicate audition for a vice presidential selection, President Joseph Biden, like an eligible bachelor with all the women at his disposal to choose from, had Senator Harris and four others - Senator Elizabeth Warren, Governor Gretchen Whitmer, and Susan E. Rice at his disposal. Just as a man's choice of a woman significantly impacts his life, any decision Mr. Biden made had a significant impact on his victory in the 2020 general election.

"It may be the most important decision they make or at least, one of the most important of their presidency, and it's the one thing that they control. But it is risky because if you make a serious mistake, it's like a bad marriage. Only you can't get a divorce."

That was a statement made by former vice president Walter Mondale. After being exhorted to cast his nets into the deep and let down his nets for other potential vice presidents, and after deliberating with his comrades for months with their great seine net but failing to find anyone, the Biden team admitted that it appeared likely that they would find anyone who would meet his requirements.

All humans are helpful or serve a purpose; however, not all humans always serve a purpose. All the women on President Joseph Biden's list were highly qualified. They were all tenderly motherly. All may have gone the additional mile at work, but Joseph R. Biden desired more. He would say I wanted a "simpatico". Like a successful marriage requires agreeable, likable shared qualities, a like-minded, sympathetic man, and a woman, President Joseph needed a "simpatico".

Believing that the woman he formerly competed against was the very candidate who made his heart smile, President Joseph Biden reasoned that not choosing Kamala Harris would be a huge mistake. Her debating skills, qualifications for office, and the racial diversity she would offer to the ticket did not become a point of contention. He just recounted the facts of the matter and then pleasantly added:

"Nevertheless, no other candidate seemed to match the political moment better."

In the end, the only candidate who scored highly with Biden's search committee on so many of their core criteria for choosing a running mate, including her ability to help him win in the 2020 November America election, was Senator Kamala Harris.

I would like every married couple to pretend they are reading aloud a portion of an autobiography they are writing about themselves; each new phase of their lives with its lofty progression.

Foreword - 1

This book is not just another book to increase the stock of books on your shelf, but it has a good spiritual insight that will help the believer to grow in grace and in the knowledge of God.

In chapter one and two, Ewuramma traces the origin of the human race and the usefulness of the scriptures.

She also handles the purpose and plan of the creation of woman; the fact that Eve's delayed creation was not a question of an afterthought but a stratagem; she does that in chapter three.

In the ensuing chapters of the book, she shares the secrets that will help all marriages to succeed.

The reader will find this a gem of a book, which he or she cannot put away, but a mine worth digging to the last depth, to deplete from it its minerals buried underneath. The reader will find in the later chapters a pool of wisdom about the family, the source of human law, how to live for the good of others, the essence of organized society and many more.

Chapter four is where Ewuramma throws light on the responsibility of the family, the place and the sacred role of the parents, and the responsibility of the children to their parents.

One will find chapter five very interesting, where Ewuramma draws parallel a mother's role and that of the church, and God's word about a nation.

In chapter 6, the subject of the two inevitable institutions are handled efficiently; how to handle the tension between the state and the church vis-a-vis the laws of God.

In the subsequent 3 chapters, the book tries to resolve the proper use of the conscience, the mystery of marriage, and the nitty-gritties of the sacred institution. The author concludes with expectations that all marriages, families, homes and churches experience an Eden to the glory of God.

This book is biblical in its underlying doctrine; though some points come from her subjective reflections of the scripture, Ewuramma has kept faithfulness to the fundamental principles of bible doctrine.

The book has a divine touch which the believer will find refreshing. I, thereforere, commend this book highly.

Yaw Adjei-Kwarteng,
Apostle, Church of Pentecost
International Executive Council Member
Area Head, Bompata Kumasi

FOREWORD - 2

Ewuramma, a member of the Church of Pentecost, Bronx District, is a known and an experienced interpreter for the Church of Pentecost, USA.

The first time I met her was when I preached at Bronx Central Church of Pentecost in 2016. She was my interpreter, and honestly, her linguistic prowess caught my rapt attention. I've had many people interpret my preachings but she stood out, with great grace, as the best for interpretation. My admiration of her linguistic potential and grace deepened when I had several one-on-one discussions with her.

Ewuramma majored in Psychology at the Stony Brook University, New York. I am, therefore, not surprised at her literary ability and her questioning expertise. She questions nearly everything constructively and thinks holistically about how to solve challenges. She is a lady with in-depth knowledge of God and the scriptures. My interactions with her gave me a strong conviction that she has garnered various pieces of information and knowledge that would be a literary treasure for generations if put into a book.

She has been an excellent student of the Holy Spirit. I had always wanted to find out how she was able to gather those pieces of in-depth knowledge to come out with this timely book, "As It Was In The Beginning". She simply told me she has held various roles in the Church in which, she thought, the Lord strategically placed her to meet different people with different circumstances so that she could gain the needed experience and knowledge in life.

Ultimately, she describes herself as a student of the Holy Spirit. Many of the things she has exquisitely explored in this book and has given expert advice on attest to the fact that she has been an excellent student of the Holy Spirit. It is remarkably interesting to note that some of the things she has given expert information and guidance about in this book are things she has not personally experienced. It simply has to be the Holy Spirit, the Excellent Teacher who has taken her through to come out with this gem of a book.

"As It Was In The Beginning" is a well thought-out and timely book. The institution of marriage is under serious attack because marriage is no longer looked upon with the lens of God but rather, it is seen in the light of what people believe is right, leading to many challenges. The Office for National Statistics for England and Wales's Divorce statistics for 2019 states that, 60% of marriages end before the 20th wedding anniversary with the average (median) length of marriage at the time of divorce being 12.2 years. The most common reason cited when people petition for divorce is "unreasonable behaviour" which covers a wide range of things, from lack of emotional support, lack of sexual relationship, refusing to contribute financially, domestic abuse and others.

This book, therefore, comes to realign the institution of marriage as ordained by God. It gives a vivid account of the origin and purpose of marriage and suggests how marriage should be re-lived. It also gives various nuggets, snippets and pieces of guidance on singlehood.

The author clearly explains the needed institutions for a successful marriage as the Family, the Church, the Society and the Government or the State. The organised duties and responsibilities of those institutions are meant to solve the challenges that distort the original purpose and establishment of marriage as ordained by God. An effective marriage in essence, depends on a strong Family, the Society, the State and the Church.

The author also places high premium on the roles of both the husband and the wife in a marriage institution. Although equal in value, men and women are not the same role-wise. The role of a man is to be the teacher, judge and administrator and to give specific instructions to specific individuals in the family in addition to making choices while the wife's role is explicitly defined as being that of her husband's companion and helpmeet in carrying out his responsibilities. Marriage is a mystery because it is re-living the relationship between Christ and His Church. The mystery is that like Christ and the Church, the two are in a covenant and each has a part to play to achieve the goals of the covenant.

The author also expounded on marriage as God's institution. The marriage institution, therefore, must always put God first. Every theory on marriage has failed except what the Lord instructed. In this book, the author details God's standards for marriage among others; as between one man and one woman as biologically defined, that a man and woman must be one flesh and that the union of marriage must be permanent and be one spouse and no more.

This book is an extraordinary tool by a gifted individual. It is an excellent resource for provoking thoughts, ideas and actions. I strongly recommend this book because it is timely, well-thought-through, insightful and ideal for training and a reference tool that will guide many in life.

Apostle George Kwaku Korankye,
London South Area, Church of Pentecost UK

Endorsements

The Author, in the book, vividly describes how God gave marriage as a gift to Adam and Eve, and hence, humanity in totality. The beauty of creation is such that God, who is perfect, made all things beautiful, and seeing how good it was, handed all His creation to man. Yet, there was the core need of man to have partnership with a *helpmeet*. Here, the writer describes the partnership of a *helpmeet* as the want of the soul. The overarching premise is "It is not good that man should be alone." *Whenever the soul has a desire that God inspires, God intends to fulfill that desire.* Hence, the creation of woman to partner man was not an afterthought of God. God perfectly did it for the continuity of the human race.

The write-up explores the trajectory of divorce and describes it as emanating from Satan and not of God. She, then, explains the need to, therefore, consider the place of solemnity in marriage ceremonies as it helps couples eschew the place of the flesh which turns to dishonor God. The book, further, counsels couples to avoid the wasted hours of promiscuous relationship so that they can embrace the nourishment and the full blessings of God in their respective marriages.

I, therefore, highly endorse this book.

Apostle Mike Kwame Etrue
Area Head, Koforidua
Executive Council Member, Eastern Regional Coordinator
Church of Pentecost

This write-up is full of insightful thoughts about God, creation, marriage, home, family, church and society. The discussion on why and how God spoke other things into existence but formed Adam from the dust is interesting. Much more interesting, perhaps, is why the Lord did not create Eve directly from the dust but from and with some body parts of Adam. The thought that this must have been done so they could be part of and complement each other, inspires discussion on home, family and society. These are developed further in the book.

This is a well-written and a pleasant reading material. Readers will find it enlightening.

Apostle Retired Joseph Kwame Assabil
Former International Executive Council Member Church of Pentecost Int.

Ewuramma has given us practical wealth of wisdom that brings health to relationships and marriage and makes us find fulfillment in life. This book is a masterpiece and a timely divine gift to the world and the body of Christ in a time that our world is woefully plagued with different worldviews and secular humanism ideologies that seek to undermine the sanctity and sacredness of marital institution against God's original intention for mankind. The author's ingenuity to beginning the book by tracing the human race to the creative power of God to reveal His purpose is remarkably espoused to enhance learning.

What sets this book apart among others is the extensive and laborious efforts put into drawing much wisdom and deepening spiritual knowledge and practical lessons about the need of mankind right from creation; the state of singlehood, the rudiments of the institution of marriage according to God's design, the bonding principles of the family unit, human laws emanating from a divine source and the need to live for the good of others as expressed in the quote:

"God's general rule is that by living for other people's welfare, we will also benefit ourselves."

The author's empathetic and compassionate tone and style of writing makes this piece a reflective book, a need assessment and a purposeful companion.

Reading through the book takes your mind through a spiritual adventure of rediscovering the purpose of God for your life and the need of mankind for the fulfillment of life. It also serves as a searchlight that throws light on deep spiritual truths; and then as a guiding light, it brings you illumination to your path for a fulfilling and lasting relationship.

Being in ministry for over 23 years, I find this book useful and a timely piece to bring illumination to both the young and the old, the singles and the married, to help them pay attention to the blueprints of God for their lives, marriages, the family units and a holistic life to enhance proper transitions in life.

Aps. Samuel Edzii Davidson,
Offinso Area Head, The Church of Pentecost

Endorsements

We are living in the times where absolute truth seems to be fading away. Everyone has their own interpretation to life. Nothing of God has the meaning to its originality. The manual or the compass of life, the Bible, has apparently been ignored. As a result of that, most people find themselves in the state of confusion. The truth is, if there is a creation, then, there must be a Creator. Nothing was created for nothing. Abusing purpose in any kind brings an untold story.

The writer, in her own small way, has suggested some antidote to this social canker by addressing the root causes of the woes of today. Get a copy for your library. This book must be read by all.

Pastor Kwasi Afoakwah-Duah
COP, Galilea District, Ghana

Questions are an important aspect of human life. It is estimated that the average person asks about 20 questions per day. We often refer to different information sources to get answers to some of life's most pressing questions about God, creation, marriage, home, family, church, and society. For instance, "Why did God form man from the dust of the ground but spoke other things into existence?"

It is refreshing that this book, with substance and simplicity, provides a coordinated intersection between those important life concepts. In this write-up, the author draws from the authoritative perspective of the Scriptures on those life issues in conjunction with everyday life lessons to simplify the otherwise complex subject of God, mankind, and our relationships.

This is a well-written and a pleasant reading material. Readers will find it both enlightening and practical. Certainly, it will be of immense benefits to all readers.

Richard Nsiah
New York District Pastor, The Church of Pentecost

I am enthused about the opportunity to read this insightful book, "As It Was in The Beginning", which talks about God, His teachings, His word and His promises.

The writer, through God's infinite wisdom, has given us a well elaborated and educative insight about relationship and marriage and how purposeful it is in the sight of God, and how relevant and essential it is in a healthy society.

Further, the book discusses three purposes of marriage - companionship, procreation and redemption. This masterpiece is a great blessing to the body of Christ and the world at large, especially the young ones who wish to journey on the part of marriage.

It educates both men and women to know their roles and place in marriage as encapsulated in Genesis 2:23: "This is now the bone of my bones and flesh of my flesh she shall be called woman because she was taken out of a man."

Not only does the book talk about marriage, but also, it talks about the origin of the human race, the church of God, the society, family responsibility and many more.

As a mother and a minster's wife, I find this spirit-filled book very useful and refreshing to all souls.

I will, therefore, entreat everyone out there to get a copy.

God bless you.

Mrs. Faustina Anane-Sarfo
Wife of Apostle Isaac Anane- Sarfo,
New York Area Head, Church of Pentecost USA INC.

CHAPTER 01

THE ORIGIN OF THE HUMAN RACE

The human race began in a family, Adam and Eve, and Eden was a home. God's creative work concluded in Adam. He was the head of all that his Creator had created. Before the creation of man, God used a formula that implies both mediate creation and generic distinction:

"And God said, Let the waters bring forth abundantly and swarm with living creatures, and let birds fly over the earth in the open expanse of the heavens" (Genesis 1:20).

God continued with His creative act:

"And God said, Let the earth bring forth living creatures according to their kinds: livestock, creeping things, and [wild] beasts of the earth according to their kinds. And it was so" (Genesis 1:24).

The formula, however, changed abruptly and beautifully when God decided to create man. He proposed direct origination as opposed to mediate origination. He no longer said, "Let the earth or the seas bring forth man", but rather, God said:

"...Let Us [Father, Son, and Holy Spirit] make mankind in Our image, after Our likeness, and let them have complete authority over the fish of the sea, the birds of the air, the [tame] beasts, and over all

of the earth, and over everything that creeps upon the earth. (Genesis 1:26).

It was no longer "after His kind" taking His typical form, and it was certainly not "after the type of a lesser creature."

God said: *"Let us make mankind in our image, after our likeness."*

Ah! All of the other creatures that God created already had partners, but man had none. However, God created Adam for society, not for solitude. So, God said:

"…it is not good (sufficient, satisfactory) that the man should be alone; I will make him a helper (suitable, adapted, complementary) for him." (Genesis 2:18).

God could have created man's companion from the same earthly dust as He had made him. But He decided to create her so that she would be a part of the man's life, bone and flesh; so that the man and woman would become more deeply and dearly united in a holy union than in any other kind of relationship:

"And the Lord God caused a deep sleep to fall upon Adam; and while he slept, He took one of his ribs or a part of his side and closed up the [place with] flesh. And the rib or part of his side which the Lord God had taken from the man He built up and made into a woman, and He brought her to the man" (Genesis 2:21-22).

Given that woman was the last creation of God's works, we can infer that she represents the pinnacle of the divine creation. And by creating a second being with human-like faculties and senses, God gave man the opportunity to learn a great deal about himself. As we leave aside everything that needs to be stated about how the divine image describes the nature and destiny of man, it would be appropriate to point out how much distinction the narrative gives Adam's origins.

There is only a fiat with the factum est - "Let it be" and "It was". It got recorded in this first narrative as to all other works of creative power. However, there is a purpose in the case of man, and that purpose is fulfilled and written in such majesty of language. To demonstrate how much emphasis the text placed on this fact, it is repeated three times, "a joyful tremor of depiction":

"So God created man in His own image, in the image and likeness of God He created him; male and female He created them." (Genesis 1:27).

As we go along in the book, we will meet details expressive of man's early state to those significant aspects of distinction in his creation, the divine council and decree concerning it, the divine type after which he was created, and the immediate divine agency exerted in his creation.

THE NEED

When the Bible is properly studied, it tells a story that is more exciting than any book because we can see in it the infinite God working with and for man. Many of the biblical stories initially appear to be a huge tangle, a snarl, or a misunderstanding. But when we examine it more closely, we realize that it is not actually a minefield but rather, an amazing arrangement demonstrating impeccable perfection and unwavering accuracy. The overarching premise is "It is not good that man should be alone."

In contrast, we see that man finds his being alone to be quite unpleasant. There is a desire at work in his heart preparing him for the blessing that God is prepared for him. Whenever the soul has a desire that God inspires, God intends to fulfill that desire. That is true of everything that the human race finds important in our world. Our hopes are often based on our desires. God, who is above and beyond His children, wouldn't put a desire in their souls unless He intended to fulfill it. In God's economy, prayer that stirs the soul is to the petitioner what a bill of goods before the payment is to a shopkeeper. God has provided prayer to His children like a basket and, then, He fills it with the blessings of His grace. Imagine Adam's feeling lonely as the earth's animals passed him by in all their natural beauty. Some people cohabit with animals like dogs and cats. They domesticate an animal and ignore their higher selves to satisfy their baser instincts. Animals may be trained to do practically anything but speak, and certain birds are endowed with the ability to speak.

Undoubtedly, Eden fit the bill. Eve was unsurprised by the serpent's talking. So, it appears she had a lengthy talk with it. Adam might have found a particular animal among the many others that would have kept him company. But he could not find anyone to fulfill his need for a helpmeet.

It is important to remember that God created man as both a social and intellectual being. Beasts can and do mate with other beasts. However, Adam's immortal nature yearned for a companion - one to communicate with, one to appreciate, one to guide, and one to see life from a different perspective. He desired someone whose thoughts should be varied but similar in their differences. He yearned for someone to help him in all aspects of life - someone he could lean on for his survival and emotional needs. Adam desired a companion who shared his personality, perspective, and destiny. He desired a partner for whom heaven would serve as a common home, and God would be a loving Father - one who could share in worship and in love with the soul. He yearned for a person who shared his passions and goals and shared his common loves, purposes, aspirations, and interests.

The first known emotion of the soul was apparently Adam's need for companionship. It comes first and stays with us the longest. In childhood, instinct and desire are usually governed wisely. Such emotions never go away. A child seeks the love of parents and the friendship of peers. The need for the loving support that God supplies to the opposite sex is felt by old age's heart which may be wrinkled just as deeply as it is by the young heart. Our perfect humanity is often incomplete without the union of a man's and a woman's souls. Even the most breathtaking sight is dull unless you can show your loved one how lovely it is. Without someone else's ability to press the cup of your pleasure, the photo gallery becomes a bit useless. Oh, how lonely it is to sip nectar from a flower of beauty that blooms in solitude only in your mind or imagination!

Even in Eden, it was not good for man to be alone. Eden was a farmland for animals before God added the woman to the man. The garden assumed a homely appearance when she came. In it, warm and adoring bowers were shown. The garden was transformed into both the entrance to heaven and God's house.

The Woman's origin is, thus, declared:

"And the rib or part of his side which the Lord God had taken from the man He built up and made into a woman, and He brought her to the man." (Genesis 2:22).

Without an Eve, a household is not an Eden since she serves as the family's beating heart. The "Home of Delights" that Eve marvelously created was exquisite, spectacular, and breathtakingly beautiful. And for many years, thoughts of her home have inspired the greatest beings on earth.

"Whenever the soul has a desire that God inspires, God intends to fulfill that desire." "Our perfect humanity is often incomplete without the union of a man's and a woman's souls."

Woman

A woman was not an afterthought to God's completed creation; God's creation was incomplete without her. Moses thoroughly recounts for her creation in the words:

"And the Lord God caused a deep sleep to fall upon Adam; and while he slept, He took one of his ribs or a part of his side and closed up the [place with] flesh. And the rib or part of his side which the Lord God had taken from the man He built up and made into a woman, and He brought her to the man." (Genesis 2:21-22).

God did not create man out of nothing as He did the physical world. He created him from earth's dust. Man is, thus, a byproduct of a previously existent substance. God's creation of the woman was also a secondary creation; nevertheless, she was made from a previously existent element. God did not create a woman out of nothing to be a thing. He intended for a woman to be more than a thing. And she must be more than a thing or she is nothingness. Thus, God created her not from earth's dust, but from a component of the freshly created man himself.

"Then Adam said, This [creature] is now bone of my bones and flesh of my flesh; she shall be called Woman, because she was taken out of a man." (Genesis 2:23).

God created the woman from "bone and flesh"—quickened dust—and thus, she is of greater quality and of better mold in her make and nature. He took the woman from man. The location from whence God took the woman holds significance. He did not take the woman from the superior part of the man in order that she would not imagine herself superior to man or endowed with the authority to reign over him. God did not take the woman from a lower part of man's body so that he would consider her inferior to himself and tread on her; but from his side—from his rib—so that she should appear equal to him; and from a place near his heart and beneath his arm, so that she might be tenderly cherished by him, and constantly be under his care and protection.

The Hebrew word interpreted as "made" means "built".

"...He built up and made into a woman, and He brought her to the man." (Genesis 2:22).

God created this woman from a man's rib. The woman contributed to the man the foundation of the home or family. A woman is built of man. Man is essential for her growth. God requires man to carry on the task that He started. He should nurture a woman, and as he does so, he improves himself.

A woman can also build. She either builds or dismantles a home. If a woman is honored in her home, she honors it. A woman is an important part of a man's life, and God depicts her role as one of equality and companionship acting freely and as an adviser. As a man recognizes in a woman the counterpart to himself, and practically his other self, a woman recognizes in a man the same counterpart to herself. She acknowledges a man as the ruler of her life, her companion, and her lover; and she is content if she finds in him her husband who suitably embraces his rights and authority.

As a man's helpmeet, a woman meets his needs as he supplies hers; she is essentially the continuation, the pouring out and pouring on of man's higher life, into the blossoms of love that decorate the home and make that chosen sanctuary the very thresholds of heaven. But unfortunately, many wives, by misinterpreting their allotted function, abuse their position as wives and become Satan's companion rather than their husband's.

Marriage

The apostles of Jesus Christ, the priests, the prophets, the judges, and the lawgivers of old had to respond to several inquiries about marriage. In those persecuted times when men frequently had to escape abruptly from their homes, they had to answer questions about whether it was preferable to remain single. The early Christians were curious as to whether it was acceptable for them to divorce their spouse supposing that spouse was already married before getting converted. The apostles had to answer many other questions on the appropriate course of action in some extraordinary circumstances. All such questions are a product of the Fall of Adam and Eve. Turning, therefore, to the Bible and to the time when it tells us there was perfectness on earth, and seeing what made man and woman happy then in Eden, we can say that the perfectness of marriage is in human adherence to the commandments of the institution of marriage as God had it. Woman is God's first gift to man.

"And the rib or part of his side which the Lord God had taken from the man He built up and made into a woman, and He brought her to the man." (Genesis 2:21-22).

God knew Eve, for he built her. He knew her heart, her mind, and her aspiration. A parent knows aspects about his or her child that no one else does. And when that knowledge is excellent and the relationship between parents and children is such that home is a place of dialogue, it is good for both parent and child.

It is, thus, the father's responsibility to give away his child—a privilege that is still in force today in true families. And every young man who desires the hand of a woman must respect that.

In that event of Eden, God set an example for parents and children to follow. The father, like God, the Father, gives the daughter's hand to her newly husband. The child, on the other hand, must prayerfully seek the approval of their parents before reaching conclusions that will determine the individual's destiny for time, and possibly for eternity.

Giving away a daughter necessitates the joy of absolute trust between father and daughter and mother and son. Blessed is the child who trusts a godly wise parent and refuses to tread a course defined by parental displeasure and disapproval. Blessed is the parent who delights in his or her child's newfound love and looks with pride and pleasure at the opening flower and ripening fruit!

After God, a woman must occupy a second place in a man's heart, or she has no place at all.

When a woman's status in a man's heart is exchanged for something or someone, both the man and the woman are shattered. It is partly in a woman's power to maintain her place next to God in a man's heart. To do so, the woman must appreciate her position, make sacrifices to maintain it and, on occasion, deny herself and bear the cross that comes with being a wife. It is hers, and God will see to it that she retains it. *"...and He brought her to Adam." (Genesis 2:23b)*

Every husband in the world should understand that his wife is a gift from God, and it is his responsibility to study and care for her. Every man may only make the woman God gives him to marry a god wife if he acknowledges that she is God-given and must be used in such a way that when the day of reckoning comes, he can give a proper account of how he has used this blessing.

Marriage, as it is, was perfect in the garden when both the man and the woman were innocent or unconscious of any practical distinction between any other commandment but God's. Adam and Eve disobeyed God, and among other penalties, God sentenced Adam thus:

"Thorns also and thistles shall it bring forth for you, and you shall eat the plants of the field" (Genesis 3:18);

and to Eve:

"…I will greatly multiply your grief and your suffering in pregnancy and the pangs of childbearing; with spasms of distress, you will bring forth children. Yet your desire and craving will be for your husband, and he will rule over you." (Genesis 3:16).

Thus, it clearly appears that the perfectness of man during his primary state was compounded by his innocence. And as someone has said: *"God will have to wash our brains before we get to heaven."* But why should I stay to prove that when we have daily proofs of it ourselves? There is so much corruption, especially in marriages, all around us worldwide.

The perfect state of mind about marriage, if it is taken in an absolute sense, can never be reinstated. There is no hope of ever regaining paradise by returning to moral ignorance or insensibility. For knowledge of good and evil cannot perish. It is indelible. It descends, of necessity, from Adam and Eve to their children in every generation. It is presented to us perpetually, and we are ever called upon at our peril to use this knowledge righteously.

"See, I have set before you this day life and good, and death and evil." (Deuteronomy 30:15).

The problem now is to re-enter Eden through this knowledge, rejecting evil and choosing good. Christ is the only substitute for the unhatched conscience of the Man of Eden. Nevertheless, given a minute study of those conditions of perfectness and their possible service in founding perfect marriage, society, and government, let us try to form a mental picture of the Man and Woman of Eden - to see their mode in the imagination of life in their delightful abode.

Humanity would have been one delightful household of brothers and sisters if it had remained in its unfallen estate. If our first parents had never sinned, we would have been one unbroken family, the home of peace, the abode of love. For God has:

"...made from one [common origin, one source, one blood] all nations of men to settle on the face of the earth, having definitely determined [their] allotted periods of time and the fixed boundaries of their habitation (their settlements, lands, and abodes)." (Acts 17:26).

No nationalities would have been divided or personal interests scattered. Nothing could have separated us. Having one common Father and Mother, one Loving Parent, and One Blissful Paradise, we would have our lives as one long heaven on earth of sweetly intermingled peace, love, joy, fellowship, and purity. One can hardly indulge a conception of such a happy world without an intense regret that the fall has made it all a dream - yet let us dream of a moment of a world where over seven billion people dwell in one big house. To do this, we must conceive of a state for argument's sake, that Adam and Eve, according to the first of all divine precepts, had increased and multiplied; and had not partaken of the tree of knowledge of good and evil; and that they and their children had continued in their blissful ignorance of sin among spontaneous and bounteous orchards - what then would have been man's life?

The Garden of Eden has a special friend in America. The nation's leadership representation in a man and a woman is a nod to how the human race began in Eden as a family. The citizenry's decision to elect a man and a woman to serve as president and vice president, respectively, has elevated the representation of marriage almost infinitely above the position it should occupy.

"...the perfectness of marriage is in human adherence to the commandments of the institution of marriage as God had it."

The Eden Home

The concept of "home" is divine in origin having originated in the mind of God, the Creator. It can only fully develop and take on its actual identity when it complies with God's original plan. God specifically designed the home to be an ideal place on Earth for man's enjoyment and usefulness. But with the man alone in the home, God saw that it was not good. The statement, *"It is not good for man to be alone"* made by God in Eden, embodies some truth that has lived with the ages and sets for an experience felt by every son of Adam. The statement, *"I will make for him a helper - suited woman - to him"*, is man's authority for the faith that somewhere on the earth God has made a helper suited to him, whom he will recognize and who will return the recognition.

There is something peculiarly impressive and instructive in producing this companion for man. She was not created simultaneously with himself. He stood alone. All other creatures had their companions and appeared in the creation male and female together. God teaches a great lesson on the importance and significance of the sacred union between a man and a woman – a lesson on the mutual dependence of those two beings on the imperfection and incompleteness of the one without the other.

It was also another lesson on the intimate and endeared relationship which was ever after to be continued between them. Hence, the woman did not appear along with the man, not until he had seen and felt alone, incomplete, and imperfect in the vast and beautiful creation about him; not until he had himself, perhaps, sighed for fellowship and companionship in his own kind. Nor, then, was a companion created for him out of the ground; that would have been cold and meaningless. It answered well enough for the transient union and intercourse of the inferior creatures; it would not have answered for the permanent, deep, and spiritual union which was to take place between these higher creatures.

The companion of the man appears under impressive circumstances. Adam sleeps, and a part of himself is taken and employed in this new creation. The Bible confirms more directly than in the hints that the woman was formed from the lowest rib of Adam, thus, from the bone and flesh of that region of the body where, as we shall see further on, the most important organs of the life of the soul are situated. So, she appeared before the man as if she had risen from his own side, from near his own heart, a companion springing up from the depths of his own life.

The man was so impressed with this wonderful production of his future companion. He recognized and felt the lesson thus:

"*Then Adam said, this [creature] is now bone of my bones and flesh of my flesh; she shall be called Woman because she was taken out of a man.*" (Genesis 2:23 AMPC).

And then, from the way in which Jesus Christ puts it, it seems God Himself broke in upon Adam's monologue and said:

"*Therefore a man shall leave his father and his mother and shall become united and cleave to his wife, and they shall become one flesh.*" (Genesis 2:24).

The force of this language is much better felt through the Hebrew than in our English version: Therefore shall she be called *Isha*, a female man—and because of this wonderful manner of creation and this tender and profound relationship to man, it shall be the tenderest and most sacred of human relations, and a man shall leave even father and mother and cleave to his wife.

Evidently, this creation of woman was not, in the estimation of either God or Adam, a mere beautiful side play but was intended for a profound and significant lesson for all coming time.

Not only did this impressive production of the woman secure this foundation of a sacred and endeared union between man and woman, but it also secured another purpose of God which he declared when he said: "*It is not good that the man should be alone, I will make a help meet for him.*" God did not mean a *helpmate* as we often hear it, but a *help meet* for him, a companion worthy of him, an associate proper for him, his equal, his counterpart, his second self, one that he can love, and in whom he can find the complement of himself, and who finds her complement in him. For in all true marriages now, as in Eden, there should not a deliberate seeking but the couple are brought to each other. Happy are those who, afterward, can recognize that the hand which led his Eve to Adam was that of an invisible God.

Man knows that it is not good for him to be alone. Separated from woman's influence, man is narrow, churlish, and brutal. Woman is a helper suited to him. With her help, he reaches a loftier stature; for love is the very heart of life, the pivot upon which its whole machinery turns without which no human existence can be complete, and with which it becomes noble and self-sacrificing.

"…for love is the very heart of life, the pivot upon which its whole machinery turns without which no human existence can be complete, and with which it becomes noble and self-sacrificing."

Family

The word family has several definitions. However, for the purposes of this book, I will only talk about two of them. The simple depiction of a family is a household where a man, the husband, a woman, the wife, children, and other dependents live together under his authority, protection, and leadership. That is how a family is represented. In one other sense, a family is defined as all people who can be related through males to a common ancestor. Usually, the word "race" describes a family of that nature.

God has only one family which is the only family in the universe. The lives of the family members are atoned for by one blood, resurrected to life by one Spirit, and recorded in one register. It is of "the whole family in heaven and on earth", not of two split families or even of a broken family. Even though its members are dispersed throughout the world, it remains one intact household.

As described in the biblical story, the household used to be an independent unit that was not a part of any other civilization. That implies that the family had everything it needed at that time. It was a society dedicated to the worship of God and the upkeep of religion; hence, it was a church.

According to William Dumbrell, the term "garden" (gan) "comes from a verb meaning "cover" or "around". That kind of a garden was an enclosed space surrounded by a wall or a hedge. While gardens are often connected with kings in the Bible and the ancient Near East, they are usually depicted as sanctuaries where priests performed service and prayer. In support of this claim, G. K. Beale makes a claim that "the Garden of Eden was the first archetypal temple in which the first man worshipped God". The garden's significance as a venue of worship stems from the fact that it validates Adam's duty as a priest. Many writers have demonstrated how many passages in Judaism actually place Adam's creation in the vicinity of the temple in Israel.

God, after creating Adam, placed him in the garden in the book of Genesis so that he could "work and guard it" - two verbs that the Torah often employs to describe the duties of the priests in the Tabernacle. Leen Ritmeyer, an expert in the architecture of ancient Jerusalem, claims that that and other analogies support the fact that the Israelite's First and Second Temples were modeled after the Garden of Eden. He makes particular use of the design of the Temples, which allowed people to enter from the east and proceed through the outer and inner courtyards before entering the Holy (which was generally only entered by priests), and from there to the westernmost part of the temple, the Holy of Holies (which the High Priest could only access on specific occasions).

A Family is God's delight. He walks in families. Walking is intended to be a special presence of love. He is present in families in a higher sense. God walks in the midst of families as a man takes pleasure in the walks of his garden. Families, like the church, are the garden of God, His Eden.

"Rejoicing in His inhabited earth and delighting in the sons of men." (Proverbs 8:31).

Like a father, God looks on this one in the family and on that — all plants of His own right-hand planting: He looks to see where the knife is wanted that He may prune the vine; or where refreshment is wanted, that He may water the roots.

Meant To Be An Edenite

There could not have been riches and poverty in the Edenic Commonwealth: no dirt, no crime, no laws, no police, no lawmakers, no kings, no soldiers, no epidemic, no pandemic, no famine, and no war. Everyone in the family was serving God; thus, nobody needed to be defended or protected by anyone.

It would have been a home without secrets, without closed doors, and locked drawers and sugar-boxes. A home where thought is free, and mind is untrammelled, is the very gate of heaven.

Eden would have been a home where the man and the woman and children are included in counsel, in love, in plan, in association. It is where children live in the presence of their parents as Abraham walked before God. The following quote add more light to it.

"I am the Almighty God; walk and live habitually before Me and be perfect (blameless, wholehearted, complete)" (Genesis 17:1).

There would have been no need for protection because every family member would have seen the other as a member of the family. Unfortunately, every disagreement, conflict, and global crisis stems from human beings' trying to avoid having to work. They are the direct and transient effects of sin. Sin, its sufferings, and labor intensity have all increased with every attempt to avoid punishment.

When a person works on anything out of necessity or personal comfort, they "create worth, price, and ownership. And those have brought upon the world a perpetual cycle of suffering, including plundering, slavery, monopoly, caste, fraud, war, conquest, and all other forms of injustices. Well, we can only crave for Edenites and move on.

CHAPTER 02

THE CHURCH OF GOD

Many people consider the Church as especially applying to the ministers, elders, deacons, deaconesses, and other officers. No one should ever believe that the Church is solely composed of preachers and elders. When you talk about the army, you are talking about all of the soldiers. Officers are sometimes mentioned first and foremost. Nonetheless, the private soldier is as important to the army as the highest officer. And so it is in the Church of God; all Christians constitute the Church. Daniel, one of the true-hearted believers who did not live for themselves, helps us to locate God's house. Daniel was a model man in the matter of a decision of character, a holy and believing man who walked before God. That "man greatly beloved" remained true to his convictions in every way. Daniel had examined the prophecies and was aware of what he had found. He applied what he had learned from the sacred Books to practical account, and discovered that a specific period was foretold in which good things would occur. Daniel set his face toward God and began to pray:

"...and for Your own sake cause Your face to shine upon Your sanctuary which is desolate" (Daniel 9:17).

Daniel did not pray for himself but for his people, many of whom were in Jerusalem, hundreds of miles away from him. Many were also scattered in various places all over the face of the earth. For them, he used that bright, sparkling eye that had looked up into the fire's supernal. He used that thoughtful and enlightened mind that had studied God's oracles for them. He used his knees, which were so intimate with the praying posture, for them. And when he was alone, he wrestled greatly, just as Jacob had. But only Daniel's pleading was for a far greater number of people who were still in direr trouble. He wrestled until he came off as more than a conqueror.

The sanctuary, the temple at Jerusalem, which Daniel referenced, is typical of the Church of God. He was speaking about THE HOLY PLACE: "Your sanctuary". He was referring to the temple at Jerusalem, which was then in utter ruin. From the time of Jesus Christ, there has been no building that was even typically holy. Jesus Christ did not attribute holiness to material substances. He did not appertain holiness to irons, stones, mortars, bricks, or timbers. He attributed holiness to the human mind and the Spirit. Sitting at the well at Sychar, Jesus Christ said to the woman of Samaria:

"A time will come, however, indeed it is already here when the true (genuine) worshipers will worship the Father in spirit and in truth (reality); for the Father is seeking just such people as these as His worshipers." (John 4:23).

So, there is still a temple on Earth, but it is not one built by human hands — a temple raised not by human masons, stone hewers, carpenters, and other artisans, but by God Himself. This temple is the Church of God. I hear someone ask: Which one among the 34,000 churches is the actual Church of God? So, where is the "church?" The truth is that there has always been just one Church, which Jesus Christ has redeemed with His own blood. God chose the living stones that make up this living temple from all throughout the world. They are being quarried one by one by effective grace and built up by the power of the Holy Spirit to become a holy temple in Christ Jesus. It was as typical as the temple in Jerusalem. There were never two temples in the same place at the same time. Truly, there was a second built upon the first's foundations. However, there was only one at a time; the second was a less spectacular continuation of the first. There was only one place in Canaan where the sacrifice could be legally presented – just one temple where people gathered for worship on special occasions. Similarly, there is only one Church of our Lord Jesus Christ.

I hear someone, again, ask:

"Which Church is that? There are about 34,000 Christian denominations in the world. Which one among the thousand is the Church of God."

The Actual Church God

Interestingly, none of the 34,000 churches is the Church of God. But there are some people who regularly assemble. They are called out by the grace of God and gathered together by the Holy Spirit. They are an assembly of faithful people who believe in the Lord Jesus Christ. The people know the truth, believe it, avow it, and adhere to it. Those persons make up the assembly of the Church of God.

The Church of God is invisible. And all the visible churches belong to the one sanctuary of God. As a result, we cannot argue that any part, or even the entire visible Church, is God's sanctuary. The visible Church serves as a shell around the true Church of God.

Some churches and people try to get a visible form of that one Church. They profess to be the one Church, but that is utterly impossible. Every attempt to comprehending all the children in one visible Church will fail. There is an invisible church here on earth. And if you ask me, "Where are they?" Or "Who are they?" I will answer:

"... The Lord knows those who are His, and let everyone who names [himself by] the name of the Lord gives up all iniquity and stand aloof from it." (2 Tim 2:19).

They are a people redeemed from the world by Jesus' specific and peculiar purchase — a people infused with one life, in whom there is only one alive and incorruptible seed that lives and abides forever: A people in mystical, real, spiritual, and indissoluble union with their great covenant Head, Jesus Christ. It is a people who are, for the most part, impoverished and unknown. Some of them, though, are in positions of power in the other family on the planet. The invisible church members are scattered up and down in the world. Some of them are strangers to one another, but Jesus Christ knows all of them. And, whether they realize it or not, they are all connected.

Adam never saw Eve until God had created her completely. No one will ever see the Church, Christ's Bride, until she is perfect and complete. When she is complete in her exquisite beauty, God shall present her to His Son, the Heavenly Bridegroom. Perfecting the Church, which is the bride, is going on every day; as Jesus Christ's Bride, she is "curiously wrought" out of material taken from His side. When all is said and done, the Church, the bride will be able to say to the groom, "Your eyes did see my substance, yet being imperfect." Jesus Christ sees, and He knows it all.

Because every true communion is with Jesus Christ, who is the Head of the invisible Church, He communes with all the rest of the members. Jesus Christ relates with all, just as every member of the body communicates with every other member. Alas, if they accidentally cut their hands, the rest of the body cannot commune with the part isolated from the body. And with time, the cut hand may die unless a surgeon ties little pieces of thread on that piece and tries to stop the blood circulation. And the heart beats through the entire body as long as there is life. Every pulse has an impact on the entire body, from the top of the brain to the bottom of the foot. So, it is with the communion of the children of God. We are all one body, and one life pervades the entire living Church of the Living God. There was only one temple and only one church.

"… There is still a temple on the earth, but it is not one built with human hands — a temple erected, not by human construction workers, but by angels, hewers of stone, carpenters, and other artificers, but built by God Himself. This temple is the Church of God."

CHAPTER 03

THE SOCIETY

Society is necessary for the well-being of man. The foundation of all governmental and social structures is the family. According to the divine plan, the head of the home should be one man who is married to one woman for life. In God's remarkable words, the union's intimacy and permanence are described thus:

"Now the Lord God said, it is not good (sufficient, satisfactory) that the man should be alone; I will make him a helper (suitable, adapted, complementary) for him." (Genesis 2:18).

The remark is true in a far broader sense than what is typically attributed to it. The connection between God's declaration and the creation of the woman demonstrates that it is most applicable to marriage and the relationship between the sexes. But it, also, implies that society is fundamental to human welfare. When God spoke of "Adam", He meant both sexes.

"He created them male and female and blessed them and named them [both] Adam [Man] at the time they were created" (Genesis 5:2).

"God blessed the man and the woman and said: "…Be fruitful, multiply, and fill the earth, and subdue it [using all its vast resources in the service of God and man]; and have dominion over the fish of the sea, the birds of the air, and over every living creature that moves upon the earth" (Genesis 1:28).

God created man to rule like a king. In his original divine state, man was superior to govern all other living things and the earth, and both were to be submissive to him. The structure of the human body and the majesty of his countenance indicate that man was created to be the lord-lieutenant of this area of creation. While the animals walk on all fours, he walks erect among them. God also pronounced a similar blessing earlier:

"...Be fruitful, multiply, and fill the waters in the seas, and let the fowl multiply in the earth" (Genesis 1:22).

Although the two blessings are similar, when it came to fruitfulness, God addressed the man and woman directly in the first blessing rather than just talking about them. God explained the second blessing by saying that it granted humans the authority or responsibility to govern the entire earth and its inhabitants. It is described as a gift or mandate from God, which is closely tied to the Divine Image in which man was created. The narrower definition is also included in the broader sense because marriage is the cornerstone of society, and women were created for it.

Man and woman give rise to the family which serves as both the foundation and raw material for all other societies. Every society's health is based on the welfare of the families that make up its members. In turn, it depends on the laws and ideologies that regulate marriage and the relationships between the sexes. It is crucial to properly understand these topics, but sadly, this is happening less and less. This is why a project like the one at hand is necessary.

Family To Community

As the first family members grow and become established, they typically choose to live close to their parents. Thus, a community made up of homes belonging to the founding family's members would quickly emerge. The need for laws to govern how individuals interact with one another then becomes apparent. As the family grows, members of the many families will need protection. Despite believing they are a part of the same family, their interests soon separate.

The head of a single household may manage without much regard for the law, but the head of multiple houses would be vulnerable to accusations of favoritism against which he would happily seek protection in norms and laws. A family-based community comprising households would feel the need for laws to control how people behave toward one another and the protection of human rights. These rights serve as the foundation for both judicial power and rights at war and peace. Therefore, that is how a family becomes the beginning of a state. Thus, a law is defined as "A rule of conduct that a superior has established and that the inferior is required to obey." The inferior would not be required to follow the rule if the superior did not have the authority to direct the inferior's behavior.

God is the only being with sovereign power and authority. His law supersedes all other laws which are obliged to take their authority from the former. No human, or a group of humans, has the right to rule over another man or to enact laws that will bind one another unless God has given them that authority. Human life is linked to God, and eternity is forever a great solemnity. God has prescribed righteousness, joy, and peace for humanity. They take pleasure in order, in symmetry, in harmony, and in proportion.

Humanity has that rule given to us in living characters in the incarnate Word if we regard the order of righteousness, peace, and joy to be in conformity with God's specified rule at the beginning.

Every human being is bound by the law which is found not in the hands of Moses but in the hands and life of Jesus Christ. It is in our best interests for every decision we make to be one that, if assessed independently and by the all-seeing God, would be righteous and conform to the flawless righteousness of Jesus Christ.

God's Law Gave Birth To Customs And Traditions

In prehistoric communities, a revelation - whether actual or imagined - usually served as the law of conduct. Traditions, which developed into usages and customs, kept it alive in both circumstances. Because they were passed down to the current generation from their ancestors, they were supposed to be in accordance with God's will. The law of God is His will. It is good, just, and holy. It is a perfect law just like its Giver. Hence, the people of old regarded it as customary law. All written legislation seems to assume and imply that this is true everywhere. And it was enforced by those who have been given authority by divine providence. This gives it the quality of a rule set by a superior that an inferior is required to follow although not in a particularly strict sense.

When the commandment of our parents and the law of the United States of America or other nations are both the commandment and the law of God, it is a very beautiful and blissful condition.

Happy are those who have both the ties of nature and the ropes of grace pulling them in the right direction.

Human Law Must Emanate From Divine Law

A family is created by marriage. Races, often known as clans or tribes, are the extension of families. They divide and come together in different ways forming a community that is not entirely of one race. By birth and aggregation, more people are added to the community. Gradually, the founding members' shared ancestry is forgotten making the group appear merely a collection of people.

The community needs authority and the rule of law when it expands beyond a family, clan, or tribe. Creating a community without rules and laws to protect it would not have been possible. They are important for safeguarding society's more vulnerable and uninformed citizens.

Legislators must make laws with authority, and that authority must come from God. Whatever name a society, a group, a hierarchy, a sect, or a company chooses to give itself, it all started in Eden as a family and a church. No matter how large, old, affluent, intelligent, pompous, prejudiced, overbearing, or exclusive it may be, it is obligated to abide by God's laws.

There is a monarchy whose power extends from the first man Adam in the Garden of Eden to "the last man", whoever that person may be. The world has one Supreme Lawmaker, one Governor, and one Judge. God hasn't abandoned creation so that its inhabitants might run it however they like without governance or a just judge. He is and He will bestow rewards and impose penalties and judgments.

Now, there are only two ways for community legislators to receive the laws of God. It might be based on a direct revelation, or it might be based on the way God has given some people graces with authority to carry out His will through the world's providential governance. Authority sometimes rests on a combination of the two things, and there is no exception to the rule.

In the case of the Church, power was initially delegated to a group of men by direct revelation, with the ability to support each other through the ongoing admission of new members. However, God providentially designates the new members. Since God does not directly impose His law through exercising His power in this world, human authority and law are essential to society.

God has enjoyed dealing with humanity as a whole, and even though He starts out with distinct individuals, He always ends up with a body of people in a covenant transaction. He leaves it up to people to uphold His laws, and for that to happen, people must understand those laws. Human laws are nothing more than guidelines established to govern those who are entrusted with upholding Divine law. God's law governs how people should behave just as His will does.

When drafting laws of the United States of America, Ghana and other nations, legislators must consider three things: God's Word, His Works, and His Providence. When His works are considered alone, it is possible to discern His will in specific situations, but it hardly provides any general guidelines.

God's general guidelines can be discovered in the Revealed Word or understood by studying God's works in relation to His providence. The ones found in the Bible are referred to as Christian Morality, Christian Laws, or Ethical Theology. The laws that can be deduced by looking at God's creation are collectively referred to as Moral

Philosophy or Natural Law since actions are seen in relation to responsibilities or rights. God never ceases to instruct. He, from heaven, brings about interesting changes in the weather and nature, not just for the benefit of the physical world but also with some thought to the inner and spiritual world.

In every action God performs, He instructs humanity and opens up to them the road to inner mysteries. Each of His actions has a peculiar gospel. God uses nature with a purpose to teach us. Nature is not only there to make us feel good. Spring, summer, fall, and winter are the four evangelists of God, each of whom offers a distinct message of the same message of divine love. Every natural phenomenon is enjoyable to the mind that strives for understanding. The naturalist never travels more than an hour without hearing the voice of knowledge unveiling the natural world. Nature is there for everyone to study and understand in the light of the Holy Spirit.

It should be noted that no system of natural law or moral philosophy that comes close to being comprehensive can be formulated without revelation.

The bible rarely provides a specific rule tailored to each unique situation; instead, on the whole, it informs us using universally applicable general concepts. It would have required more than an entire library than one Bible to address every individual moral emergency that might arise and resolve every individual issue of conduct. For those who the Spirit of God instructs, general truths are far more precious to them than specific commandments. It is easier to apply a general concept to an unusual circumstance than it is to determine exactly what the unique case may be and what the special rule applicable to it is. I am, therefore, partially doubtful that this is true for everyone.

"In every action God performs, He instructs humanity and opens up to them the road to inner mysteries."

WE MUST LIVE FOR THE GOOD OF OTHERS

All laws must be upheld and given legal interpretation. God has established three sorts of communities for those reasons, and it is His wish that everyone belonged to one of these communities. The fall damaged every single human ability or capability. While our judgment was changed from its natural balance, the will was corrupted, and the affections were tainted. More of the integrity and strength of the human memory was lost. Thus, it makes sense why we remember evil more clearly than good. However, God has not left it up to humanity to extrapolate His law. He grants the ability to explain His law to those He selects under the direction of the Holy Spirit. The householder asked:

"Am I not permitted to do what I choose with what is mine? [Or do you begrudge my being generous?] Is your eye evil because I am good?" (Matthew 20:15).

Even so, God poses the same question. Among others, no characteristic of God gives Him more entitlement than Divine Sovereignty. Unquestionably, God has not treated all men equally when it comes to material things. He has not given all of His beings the same number of graces or place in creation. There is a distinction. He has graciously met some people on His own domain, dealt with them on His own terms, and given them what they need to contribute to society's development. Apostle Paul speaks about those on whom God bestows His gifts.

"Therefore it is said, When He ascended on high, He led captivity captive [He led a train of [a]vanquished foes] and He bestowed gifts on men." (Ephesians 4:8).

God, through Jesus' ascension, bestows gifts on humanity, not on angels, not on devils, on men only - poor fallen men. Paul does not say "for priests or ministers" but "for men." Nonetheless, a unique character is mentioned. Paul does not particularly mention "Saints" or "Sinners". What wonderful sovereignty there is in God's grace! He truly does what pleases Him, as evidenced by the following:

"...has mercy on whomever He wills (chooses) and He hardens (makes stubborn and unyielding the heart of) whomever He wills" (Romans 9:18).

God, if He so chooses, may kill two birds with one stone. By bestowing gifts on all of humanity, He gives both saints and sinners a profitable theme for thought. There is but one gospel message and it has a voice for all. Saints know no sweeter music than the name of Jesus, and sinners know no richer comfort than His person and His work. God bestows His gifts to all when He gives Jesus Christ who is all in all. Jesus comes as life to the dead and is equally life to the living.

God can make presidents, senators, pilots, priests, etc., of those who have sinned as drunkards. He makes loyal friends out of those who have broken His laws of purity, truth, and honesty. God's description of bestowing gifts includes people who have rebelled against God while once professing to be His devoted subjects. When Jesus Christ ascended to the highest place possible, He remained the sinner's friend. When all His pains and grief were being rewarded with endless horror, He turned His eye upon those who had crucified Him and bestowed gifts upon them. Would you not turn to the God who so loved you?

"For God so greatly loved and dearly prized the world that He [even] gave up His only begotten ([d]unique) Son, so that whoever believes in (trusts in, clings to, relies on) Him shall not perish (come to destruction, be lost) but have eternal (everlasting) life" (John 3:16).

God's general rule is that by living for other people's welfare, we will also benefit ourselves. God requires that we live for others rather than just our own interests.

"The liberal person shall be enriched, and he who waters shall himself be watered." (Proverbs 11:25).

If you ask, politicians, doctors, the clergy, philosophers, physicians, sociologists, psychologists, teachers, pilots, drivers, or sweepers: what practical ends or results they expect from all their research and meditations. If they know what they are about, they will answer: they aspire to Goodness; Goodness for themselves, Goodness for the rest of humanity. It will be said of a physician that they have a small intellect and selfish feelings if they only work on themselves and their immediate family after completing years of medical school.

A priest does not establish a church for himself and his family alone. Neither does a president rule over his or her family only. None of them seek their own comfort, distinctly and independently, dismissing all care or consideration for the goodness of others or the United State of America. With an enlarged mind, seeing that there is no severance from society, they know that the only avenue to private Goodness is through public Goodness.

The analogy of nature upholds their conduct. An unwritten rule in nature says nothing can exist independently of everything else. An action and a reaction have a mutual impact on every other action. Invisible cords connect all of the elements that make up the universe. No single organism exists there that emanates, grows, or decomposes for itself. Even though the planets are far apart, they are attracted to one another, and although appearing to be incomparably far away, the fixed stars are, nevertheless, connected to one another by unfathomable bonds.

God created the universe in such a way that selfishness is the gravest imaginable violation of His law. He has arranged things so that serving others and living for them is the strictest form of submission to His will.

Therefore, those God divinely appoints are to essentially paraphrase His laws when they pass laws for the nation. Instead of verbatim recitation of God's laws, they give the laws they enact for the people significance by including the interpretation of God's law. Their laws and interpretations may be taken as authoritative when they speak while under the direct influence of the Spirit of God's law. God's Spirit is the one who truly understands what He means when He gives humans His laws. Legislators may not have all meant the same things, but the Spirit's meaning must still prevail.

"God's general rule is that by living for other people's welfare, we will also benefit ourselves."

The Essence Of An Organised Society

Society must be organized because it has duties. 'Organized', 'direct', 'set straight', 'appointed', 'firmly established', and 'rightly framed society' are potential translations. Anyone who has had the opportunity to witness an army of locusts marching will be awestruck by the amazing regularity of their procession.

"The locusts have no king, yet they go forth all of them by bands." (Proverbs 30:27).

It is amazing that creatures that are very small in stature and low on the intellect scale can preserve more than just a strict sense of order during their long flights and vicious marches. Regarding the journey and research of life, there are two extremes. Some argue that humans don't require any kind of leadership. They claim that humans are honorable beings endowed with great intelligence. We have the ability to think, judge, understand, and discern. We can certainly navigate ourselves without outside guidance. We do not require a teacher because we are capable of teaching ourselves as learners. I have no problems with any of those except that no matter how noble we may be, it has never been simple for humans to establish order on our own. I think we would not be intelligent beings if we always agreed on everything; there is plenty of legitimate disagreement among us. There are many people, nonetheless, who do not even have order among the parts of their own bodies. They are unable to govern themselves. Their nuclear families are, therefore, chaotic. There are occasionally the most unpleasant conflicts and arguments in many large families and even in small ones.

And a happy household with a good leader is one that is completely organized. There are visible signs of discord and strife everywhere, including the world's various corporations, institutions, and associations. Reports of the disputes in the various churches, legislators that meet in the House of Representatives, or senators and congressmen that meet in the parliament dominate television news and newspapers.

Even if we could take all of humanity to a place of orderliness, love, peace, and unity, it would be difficult to keep certain individuals there. Peace, love, unity, and orderliness reside halfway between two extremes, and our perception swings far too much in either direction. Except by the grace of God, we never find those important qualities at the center of knowledge, understanding, and wisdom. Instead, we swing from side to side rather than staying still for very long.

Since the fall of man, it has been clear from our actions toward one another and ourselves that we desperately need a moral and spiritual leader. We require many, not one. An animal conducts its inherent functions using the organs that make up its body. Therefore, the officials of a society through whom it carries out its operations may be referred to as its organs. There should be a very close, very loving, and very total unity between all the organs.

All work that benefits our society is honorable. An honest profession never needs to be embarrassed of by anyone whether they work as a potter, a farmer, or in any other profession. The worker need never feel ashamed about the skill or work that went into earning their fair compensation.

"In the sweat of your face shall you eat bread until you return to the ground, for out of it you were taken; for dust you are and to dust you shall return" (Genesis 3:19).

In humble, sincere labor, there is always an honor and some dignity as well. Even the Bible does not shun mentioning the name of the lowly profession: shepherd, carpenter, farmer, tent maker. It is regarded as desirable to be a king or the president of a nation. People that perform those tasks are entitled to some respect from their contemporaries. Even common work done properly is considered deserving of its pay, but work performed for a whole citizenry typically has something unique to commend it. The media goes to great lengths to inform us that those people are honored to serve their country by appointment or election. It airs on national and occasionally on international televisions. It appears on newspaper front pages.

On billboards, they are designated as "The President-Elect" or "The King or Queen Enthroned". Presidency and Royalty appear to elevate them. However, it is important to remember that society is made up of a variety of distinct organs. Therefore, it would be the height of foolishness for one organ to tell another "You are a-nobody because you are unable to carry out the duties that I have been called to do. So, you are useless".

Each organ needs to rejoice for its neighbor. One who is appointed to a position must fill it, and while they should sympathize with friends who hold other positions, they should never elevate themselves above their friends.

Such officials and laws that specify, distribute, and set boundaries on their authority are necessary for a society with responsibilities. These guidelines give it some structure and make it an ordered society. As I mentioned earlier, three categories or types of societies are organized and have been granted authority by God. It seems to be God's intention that every person belongs to a specific organization within each class. Within its respective domains, each has authority over its own members. A given society can exist in a variety of ways without losing its status as a member of its right class. Each of the three classes was founded for a particular purpose: families to oversee children's education and training to enhance both their temporal and spiritual health; churches to oversee men's spiritual wellbeing; and governments to oversee their material welfare.

It is safe to state that the head of the organs of the society who leads is highly important to the health of the nation. Accidents can cause people to lose a foot, a leg, an arm, an eye, or an ear. It is quite amazing how they can still live even after losing many of their parts. But if their head is cut, they will not survive. The body that has had its head severed from it instantly dies. Therefore, if the head of a nation's organs is unhealthy, the laws of God cannot flow through her to all of her citizens, and that will cause the society to collapse and eventually die.

Organized societies vary widely in terms of the number of members, the area of the territory they occupy, and the tenets that govern the membership.

In each scenario, the family's power is extended to a small group of largely related people residing in the same home. The plan fails anywhere that attempts are made to push the family's power considerably beyond these bounds. Society must be structured according to values that are incompatible with the values of the family in order that it appears successful.

Everyone who lives in a particular area governed by the United State of America is subject to her authority. It may be big or small, populated or not, but it is considered that those who live there constitute a community. That means they share a set of values and moral codes. America's, Ghana's or any other country's duly elected officials represent the community. They have control over the group's constituents, the area it inhabits, and anything that is found there.

*"It is safe to state that the head of the organs
of the society who leads is highly important
to the health of the nation."*

"THE SOCIETY"

In addition to the three organizations that have already been discussed, each of which has a purpose, function, and organ, every community may be taken into account under a fourth phase. It is known as Society. In this view, society lacks organs and consequently has no functions. It is often described as being organized; the phrase "social organization" is well-known; yet, it simply refers to periodic arrangement. Society is organized into classes, orders, grades, cliques, circles, coteries, trades, professions, and what are referred to as "worlds" which are groups of people that share similar preferences, habits, and ways of thinking. A person may be a member of more than one division because each of these groups contains a large number of members who are also included in other divisions.

The same community's political and religious institutions are greatly impacted by this arrangement which, in turn, has an impact on them. Those institutions then respond to the social arrangement also known as the social organization. It is even asserted that society, in the sense in which the word has just been used, has organs, or at least some of its divisions do. However, what are referred to as organs are not actually organs. They are the only people, or perhaps periodicals, who voluntarily take it upon themselves to speak for society as a whole without being given permission to do so, perhaps in an effort to furthering certain interests or disseminating certain viewpoints. Public opinion is very important since it determines how society functions. It makes an effort to modify, override, and even change the law of America, Ghana or any country, the law of the Church, and even the law of God.

It develops in this way: Every one of society's different divisions, which it may be easy to group together under the umbrella term of classes, has its own manners, customs, and morals that are tailored to the advancement of its own interests, and shapes its public opinion. Each of those classes has taken morality into its own hands insofar as it affects its interests and has unofficially established a code of morals. One of those codes — known as Public Opinion — was created by general society from those other codes.

By rubbing up against one another, it modifies the particular codes by adopting and enforcing their observance. Although it hardly acknowledges the existence of the Divine rule and practically pays little or no heed to its principles, it subtly claims to be an explication of it. All of the different classes' codes clearly prefer class interests. Therefore, even if they do not break Christian law, they fall short of it. Nevertheless, they are all accepted as a part of the overall consensus of public opinion; sometimes, even when they are blatantly in conflict with the public good.

Every class is prepared to ignore the vices in the codes of other classes in the hopes that those of its own would likewise be disregarded. Some truisms and rules that apply to people's interactions in general, regardless of other relationships, are added to the specific codes. That was how the public opinion moral code came into being. It is created by society in its disorganized state, which is evaluated independently of the three organizations that God has established. That society imposes a penalty for it in the form of social exclusion or humiliation. Because the people who make up society are corrupt by nature, society cannot be, otherwise, dysfunctional or corrupt. History has consistently demonstrated that attaining perfection does not increase with the presence of several flawed beings. Society has the power to enforce its laws, and it uses that power without hesitation.

Although it has no direct gift of authority in the Divine law, it has some right to exist because it was given permission to wield power in the course of Divine providence. It makes no such claims of rights or any other kind of legal authority; it just makes claims of power. In spite of this, society has the right to be heard, subject to demands of individual conscience to compare its rules to the Divine law or to the righteous human laws of the Church and the State. However, private conscience in this situation is just as hesitant and delayed acting as private judgment is in church affairs.

People also take a long time challenging the legal system by turning to their own discretion or conscience. Both of those occurrences have the same cause: the general public is more afraid of civil and social punishments than they are of church disciplinary measures. Anyone who is outside of her area or does not wish to do so is not subject to punishment. Exclusion is, therefore, the ultimate penalty for the Church.

However, all people are afraid of penalties, incarceration, and the ridicule of those they associate with. Public opinion has grown to be quite influential. It occasionally imposes state legislation and occasionally prohibits their application. It has an excessive and harmful effect within the Church, which manifests more through the prevention of proper enactments than the instigation of bad ones. It negatively impacts on how discipline is enforced. It is unlikely that public opinion can positively impact the Church because it is, itself, unsound and does not understand or know the values of the Church.

The three distinct groups or classes of groups to which authority has been divinely committed are the Family, the Church, and the State. Every human is born into a family and, in most cases, should remain a part of that family throughout their lives as either the head or a member. However, in some cases, God, through the use of His Providence, may relieve a person from this duty by making compliance impossible. Every person should become a member of the Universal Church and communicate with it through the local church where they already attend services. Within the boundaries of every State in the world in which they reside, every individual is required to submit to the authority of the State; it is up to them whether they choose to do so or not. Those three entities have the authority to pass laws and [appoint] governors who draft and carry out their legislation. They were put in place to accomplish three separate goals. All of humanity is to have their eternal needs met by the Church.

CHAPTER 04

FAMILY RESPONSIBILITY

The Family is responsible for educating its members to meet both groups' needs. Both the Church and the State are divinely established institutions, and the families and individuals that make up each are connected to them in ways other than through voluntary associations.

The internal structure of the family has been made the subject of direct revelation; all power is given to the head which is the father if there is one, or the mother.

"Regard (treat with honor, due obedience, and courtesy) your father and mother, that your days may be long in the land the Lord your God gives you" (Exodus 20:12).

Apostle Paul rehearsed the same words in a broader way when he said:

"Children, obey your parents in the Lord [as His representatives], for this is just and right. Honor (esteem and value as precious) your father and your mother—this is the first commandment with a promise — That all may be well with you and that you may live long on the earth. Fathers do not irritate and provoke your children to anger [do not exasperate them to resentment] but rear them [tenderly] in the training and discipline and the counsel and admonition of the Lord." (Ephesians 6:1-4).

Such instructions forbid any doubt as to the family's internal structure. It is a monarchy, and the only internal limits on the monarch's power are those within his or her heart. However, the constitution itself restricts his or her power even though it doesn't offer any external method to keep him or her inside those restrictions. There are other texts that are closely related to those that have been cited as providing the head of the family authority and govern how that authority is used.

"Husbands, love your wives, as Christ loved the church and gave Himself up for her, So that He might sanctify her, having cleansed her by the washing of water with the Word, That He might present the church to Himself in glorious splendor, without spot or wrinkle or any such things [that she might be holy and faultless]. Even so, husbands should love their wives as [being in a sense] their own bodies. He who loves his own wife loves himself" (Ephesians 5:25-28).

All the above scriptures and many more adequately demonstrate God's restriction on the authority bestowed by the others. It is that kind of tender affection that He has ordained to be the inevitable outcome of family relationships in His infinite knowledge and goodness. The small size of the community produces strong feelings of attachment, the shared interests of its members, their closeness, and their continuous sharing of benefits. The head shares those emotions and is given a check against the abuse of power which must always be present in such institutions. In the event that this check proves to be lacking or insufficient, the power of America or other State and the church serve as backup measures. The family is now a subservient society where the head and each member are subject to the authority of the other members. The higher authority of the Church and the State serve as external checks on the power of the family's patriarch and matriarch.

THE ROLE OF FAMILY HEAD

Without the limitations of legislative oversight, the male or female monarch under a family monarchy possesses administrative and judicial authority. They have the authority to impose laws that their subordinates must follow. These laws are or ought to be interpretations of God's law; nevertheless, they are unable to establish any regulations for the executive or judicial branches because they alone have the power to execute all executive and judicial functions. Because they are the lone judge, they will very rarely set any regulations; instead, they will interpret the Divine law as needed on the spot. Their decisions, which over time will be seen as a sort of usage or customs of the family, might be used by others to infer the guiding principles on which they base their actions.

As a teacher, a judge, and an administrator, they will also give commands, directions, or instructions to specific individuals in addition to making choices. These might also be incorporated into the family's traditional or customary law. This type of government, as mentioned earlier, is known as paternal government. The leader of a family is subject to the laws of the Church and State and must consider them while interpreting the Divine Law. Within the Church and the State's separate areas, the teacher, the judge or the administrator must adhere to their views; nevertheless, they are free to make their own interpretations in the morality-related field. However, they will probably overuse the power of the general public's opinion in this situation.

The opposition to private judgment will, somewhat, embarrass the head of a family in his work of interpretation because a sizable section of his subjects lacks the ability to form views and are, therefore, devoid of any private conscience that would be allowed to be taken into account. His government has a peculiar personality as a result of this fact, the confines of his jurisdiction, and the lack of any parliamentary checks. All of his methods of operation are informal. He makes up his mind and begins to declare or carry out his decision after consulting with the family members he chooses. In the event that the case has a judicial bent, he may, at his discretion, completely disregard or sparingly employ the forensic forms. His overall love for every individual under his control makes everything bearable.

Focus Of Parental Guide

This paternal government performs beautifully in the family because its primary goal is to increase the well-being of the people it governs. But because the paternal concern is not sincere, that form of government never works in America or in most counties. The tenderness of parental love and the similarity of interest that ties the leader of a family and its members together do not serve to restrain the exercise of power. The parent's highest joy is their children walk in truth. They have no greater joy:

"I have no greater joy than this, to hear that my [spiritual] children are living their lives in the Truth" (3 John 4).

And it's worth-noting that this joy is unique to Christian fathers and mothers. No parents can say from their hearts, "We have no greater joy than to hear that our children walk in truth" unless they are, themselves, walking in truth. No tiger prays for its offspring to become a rat. The ungodly man sets small stores by the godliness of their children since they think nothing of it for themselves. They that do not value their own soul are not likely to value the souls of their descendants. They that reject Jesus Christ on their own account are not likely to be enamored of Him on their children's behalf. Abraham prayed for Ishmael, it is not recorded in the bible ever that Ishmael prayed for his son Nebajoth. I fear that many, even professors of religion, could not truthfully repeat John's words. They seek delight in their children and are unconcerned about whether or not they are walking in truth. They rejoice in their children if they are physically well, but they are not saddened if the leprosy of sin stays on their offspring. They take pleasure in their (children's) attractive appearance to human and do not wonder whether they have found favor in the eyes of God. Many family heads will meet all of their children's material needs. They buy everything the child asks but never inquire if they chose the wide or narrow road. It is heartbreaking to watch how some professedly Christian parents are content as long as their children demonstrate intelligence in learning or business acumen while displaying no symptoms of a regenerated character.

If they pass their exams with honor and promise to be well-equipped for the wars of the physical world, their parents forget that there is a superior war involving a higher crown for which the child must be fitted by divine grace and armed with the entire armor of God. If our children do not receive the crown of life, it will be a paltry consolation that they have received the honors of schools and organizations. Many people who should know better believe that their children are exceptionally privileged if they become wealthy, marry well, start profitable businesses, or achieve eminence in the career that they have chosen. Their parents will go to bed joyful and arise completely satisfied, even if their lads are speeding down to hell if they are also making money by the bushel.

They have no higher joy than seeing that their children are living their lives and storing treasure where rust can spoil it. Some parents are content with their children's waywardness circumstances despite the fact that they show no signs of the new birth, no indication of being rich toward God, no signs of loving favor, redeeming grace, or the regenerative power of the Holy Spirit. With humility and through the mercies of God, I simply say to such professing parents that they must consider whether they are Christians at all, and if they will not, they must allow the word of God to do so.

When a person's heart is really right with God, and they themselves have been saved from the wrath to come and are living in the light of their heavenly Father's countenance, it is certain that they are anxious about their children's souls, prize their immortal natures, and feel that nothing could give them greater joy than to hear that their children walk in truth. Judge yourselves, then, beloved, by the gentle but searching test of this information. If you claim to be a Christian but cannot say that nothing brings you more joy than the conversion of your children, you should reconsider making such a claim in the first place.

"They that do not value their own soul are not likely to value the souls of their descendants."

THE STATE IS GOD ORDAINED

America, Ghana or any other nation is a divinely appointed institution just like the Church and the Family. It does not, however, have a form that was predetermined by God. The government is responsible for the well-being of the people. Everyone agrees with this statement despite the argument that it is occasionally still portrayed as a necessary evil. That phrase's underlying meaning, which is concealed, is that it's an unpleasant good. It was formerly widely believed that the conclusion to be drawn from it was that the best government was the one that regulated the least.

It was a blatant misrepresentation of the truth similar to many other widely accepted ideologies. The truth is that any limitation the government imposes on private citizens must have a very good reason. Government is a God-ordained institution because man cannot exist without it. Thus, by applying human intelligence to God's works and providence, much can be learned from the light of nature.

"Let every soul be subject to the higher powers. For there is no power but of God: the powers that be are ordained of God. Whosoever, therefore, resists the power, resists the ordinance of God: and they that resist shall receive to themselves damnation. For rulers are not a terror to good works, but to the evil. Wilt thou then not be afraid of the power? Do that which is good, and thou shalt be praised. For he is the minister of God to thee for good. But if thou do that which is evil, be afraid; for he bears not the sword in vain; for he is the minister of God, a revenger to execute wrath upon him that doeth evil. Wherefore ye must need be subject, not only for wrath but also for conscience' sake." (Rom 13:1-5 KJV).

Even though it is often overlooked, this passage is rich in wisdom, and it is safe to argue that it serves as the foundation for the entire field of political science. There is nothing about organizational structure or political theory in it. Thomas Jefferson and Thomas Paine reject both the majority's natural right and the divine right of monarchs of Sir Robert Filmer. The Bible supports neither of those. It is believed that the existing authorities have the authority to rule.

God has placed in men the ability to enforce order through His providence. They must be obeyed since failing to do so would be against a divine command:

"Submit yourselves to every ordinance of man for the Lord's sake: whether to the king, as supreme; or unto governors, as unto them that are sent by Him for the punishment of evildoers, and for the praise of them that do well. For so is the will of God, that with well doing ye may put to silence the ignorance of foolish men: as free, and yet not using your liberty for a cloak of maliciousness, but as the servants of God." (1 Pet 2:13-16 KJV).

The Apostles established the broad rule that every governmental ordinance must be obeyed. Apostle Peter used the government in which he and the people to whom he was writing directly lived to demonstrate the idea as seen in the following:

"Be submissive to every human institution and authority for the sake of the Lord, whether it be to the emperor as supreme" (1 Peter 2:13).

The writer of the book of Romans followed the principle into some of its important consequences. He first tells his readers that the authority of the United States of America, Ghana or any other country extends to all persons.

"Let every person be loyally subject to the governing (civil) authorities. For there is no authority except from God [by His permission, His sanction], and those that exist do so by God's appointment." (Romans 13:1).

Next, it extends to the infliction of capital punishment, and by a parity of reason, to making war.

"If thou do that which is evil, be afraid; for he bears not the sword in vain; for he is the minister of wrath upon him that doeth evil. "Let every person be loyally subject to the governing (civil) authorities. For there is no authority except from God [by His permission, His sanction], and those that exist do so by God's appointment. Therefore, he who resists and sets himself up against the authorities resists what God has appointed and arranged [in divine order]. And those who resist will bring down judgment upon themselves [receiving the penalty due them]. For civil authorities are not a terror to [people of] good conduct, but to [those of] bad behavior. Would you have no dread of him who is in authority? Then do what is right and you will receive his approval and commendation." (Romans 13:1-3)

There is a restriction inherent in all of that power. Rulers have the authority to determine what actions are evil, but they must have a standard by which to do so. Because the ruler is God's minister, and must submit to God's will alone, who is the only source of their authority, the rule is God's law. Therefore, all laws made by humans are merely expositions of the law of God. They might be incorrect and even go against the rule of God. People must dismiss them when they do not comply with it, which is very different from opposing the power that enacts them *"… We must obey God rather than men." (Acts 5:29)*

Private conscience has the authority to make decisions in certain situations, but it must do so in accordance with established guidelines. Once more, the purpose of the State is to advance the physical well-being of people who are under her control. It has nothing to do with the condition of men's souls. The spiritual health of a person depends on their interior state which cannot be changed by any external powers, and the state's powers are all external religious practices performed out of respect for human laws that are not acceptable to God. Faith is not simply conforming to religious observances on the outside.

Religion is made up of faith and obedience, but they must be based on the person of Jesus Christ and God's commandments, respectively. Since the State is unable to influence a person's religious beliefs and obedience to God's law, she lacks the authority to meddle in their religious observances, and her actions on religion are not binding on a person's conscience.

"Then Peter and the apostles replied, We must obey God rather than men" (Acts 5:29).

The major restriction on America, Ghana or any other nation's power is that she cannot excuse any man from committing a sin. Private conscience should determine what constitutes sin, with the law of God serving as the standard.

Man's Duty Is To Worshhip God

A living human must "serve the living God" in order to be happy; this is why we were created, and if we do not revere our Creator, we will fail to fulfill the purpose of our creation. The primary objective of man is to exalt God and enjoy Him forever. If we fall short of that goal, we are the real losers. The only element in which we may truly live is in the service of God. A fish cannot survive on dry land. Even if it were able to survive on dry land, it would lead an incredibly terrible life and hardly even be a fish! It wouldn't get the chance to realize its full potential, and nobody would know what it was capable of. The fish does not become a fish and begin enjoying its life until you throw it into the river. It is exactly the same for humanity: if we live without God, we should not even try to term that condition "life":

"...he who believes in (has faith in, clings to, relies on) the son has (now possesses) eternal life. But whoever disobeys (is unbelieving toward, refuses to trust in, disregards, is not subject to) the Son will never see (experience) life, but [instead] the wrath of God abides on him. [God's displeasure remains on him; His indignation hangs over him continually.] shall not see life, but the wrath of God abides on him." (John 3:36).

Even though we try to live a life of pleasure, we are already dead. We are designed in such a way that if we want to fully develop as God intended, we must get glued to His fellowship and to serving Him. Unfortunately, since the fall of man, we have wandered and violated our consciences, rendering them heartless. Therefore, we do not truly see the loss of a sense of God's presence. A heartless conscience carries a powerful curse.

Human nature has evolved into being like a lake of mischief. How destructive and cold-hearted the water is! Then, after creating thousands of widows and orphans, it smiles as if nothing has happened! When human nature is unleashed, it causes massive damage! Instead of talking about how terrible the list of harms created by human nature is, I want you to think about how many lives are injured as a result of other people's nature. What destruction so many people have caused by continuing to act immorally and wickedly! How many people who set out on their life's journey and wished themselves well for a safe passage have hit the rocks because of other people!

Many precious lives have been lost and destroyed as a result of unfavorable rumors, careless remarks, nefarious deeds, and cunning schemes. Conscience can fill in the blanks and save us from being abandoned, which would otherwise lead to chaos for ourselves! No punishment that I can think of is more detrimental to a person's soul than when God allows them to do things their own way. *"Let him alone he is joined to idols";* and if the Lord says that, there is only one other word more dreadful, and that is the final sentence - *"Depart from me, ye cursed, into everlasting fire, prepared for the devil and his angels."*

When God abandoned Pharaoh to his hardness of heart, it was a severe punishment for his arrogance and brutality. Alas! Conscience does not always speak in the same tone or with the same intensity in every person. Conscience can be tied like a dog preventing it from biting the sin thief.

Many people have varied perspectives about God's watch. Because their conscience never stops correcting them, they still believe that God is watching them. Since they are unable to approach God due to their sin, they do not see any laws to stand in the way of their fellowship with Him.

However, some people have inherently sensitive consciences, and sin is never easy for them. They have a swollen conscience, much like someone who has lost their voice owing to a sore and swollen throat brought on by a cold. Even after years of wrongdoing and criminal activity, some people might sense that God's providence is working against them in addition to being disturbed by conscience and suffering from agony.

They may make an effort to having a good time all day because they believe it to be one of the best things to chase dreary fear away, but dreary fear, like chickens, returns to the roost at night. It is noteworthy that this is not the case with everyone.

*"A living human must "serve the living God"
in order to be happy; this is why we were created,
and if we do not revere our Creator,
we will fail to fulfill the purpose of our creation."*

The Church Plays A Spiritual Role

God has entrusted another organization with the handling of religious matters. In comparison to America, Ghana or any other nation and the Family, the Church differs in that the Divine Word only partially prescribes the structure of her organization. It was established for a reason other than the one the State was created to fulfill.

Her mission is to strengthen humankind's spiritual well-being. People's spiritual health is dependent on their faith and obedience which must be active and internal rather than merely formal and external. The Church cannot use external force to resolve internal issues; instead, she must deal with them. She is not able to force anyone to join her.

She might create regions of the world for specific denominations, which would act as missionary organizations to convert everyone living in their respective regions. When someone joins the church voluntarily, or their parents place them under their authority because they cannot act for themselves, the church will have ecclesiastical jurisdiction over them. The church lacks the legal authority and resources to compel acquiescence, and the state, which has the resources, is not authorized to intervene.

Each person who joins the Church must do so voluntarily. This is apparent from the character of the Church which was established exclusively for spiritual purposes, and from the ways in which she is the only one who may impose her authority. So long as a person belongs to the Church, they are required to respect her authority. However, the only means she has to enforce obedience is discipline and in extreme situations, excommunication or exclusion from her sphere of authority.

Monarchy / The Roles Of The Arms Of Government

The leaders of families do not have the same authority as the heads of the other two groups. The powers of government are typically broken down into three categories: The legislative branch is responsible for creating proposed laws, approving or disapproving presidential nominations for the Supreme Court, judges of the federal courts, and heads of federal agencies. It also has the power to declare war. The executive branch executes and upholds legislation. The president, vice president, Cabinet, executive departments, independent agencies, and additional boards, commissions, and committees are all included in this. The judicial branch determines whether laws are constitutionally flawed, applies the law to specific situations, and determines the interpretation of legislation. The Supreme Court and other federal courts are included in it.

"Let every person be loyally subject to the governing (civil) authorities. For there is no authority except from God [by His permission, His sanction], and those that exist do so by God's appointment".

The distinctions between these sorts of powers are taken seriously in America and, to some extent, in the Church, but they are overlooked in families. Because of this, a government is referred to as paternal if it neglects its citizens while claiming to act in their best interests but disregards them. Using the United States as an example, the primary responsibility of the legislative branch, represented by the US Congress, is to enact laws for the nation. The Senate and the House of Representatives are the two chambers of Congress. Each state's citizens elect a member of Congress to represent it in the federal government. Each state has two senators; however, the number of representatives a state has depends on her population. There are 435 elected representatives in the House of Representatives, 100 senators, and 6 non-voting delegates who represent the District of Columbia, Puerto Rico, and other American territories. Both houses must approve a bill for it to become law. The president can either sign the bill into law or veto it if both houses of Congress approve it.

The executive branch's responsibility is to carry out the laws of the country. The president is in charge of the executive branch and serves as the military's commander-in-chief. He or she is also in charge of signing or vetoing laws that Congress sends to the executive branch. The vice president who presides over the Senate if the president cannot carry out his or her duties, and the Cabinet which serves as the president's counselors, are also included in the executive branch. Several federal agencies and departments often carry out the enforcement of laws in the executive branch.

The judicial branch is responsible for assessing laws and determining whether citizens adhere to the guidelines established by the Constitution. The Supreme Court, which has nine justices, is the highest court in the country. A case must proceed through the legal system until it is appealed to the Supreme Court from a lower court before the Supreme Court would hear it. The president nominates, and the Senate confirms the judicial branch's members.

CHAPTER 05

THE CHURCH IS A MOTHER

She always stands in that relationship with all her members. When you take each member of the Church individually, they are a child of the Church. And when you combine all of them altogether, they make up the mother, the CHURCH. A mother loves her own child, especially because it is her own. She watches over it with sedulous care; she denies her eyes the necessary sleep at night if her babe is sick, and she would be ready to die in the stead of her child. You may give a nursing mother another person's child and pay her a huge sum of money to induce her to love the child. Try as the mother may, she cannot transfer her affection to the other child. However, the mother's own child is exceedingly precious to her. She can easily love her as she breathes air in and out.

As a mother, the church, by her motherly love, keeps her children in her bosom. She puts them on her lap and cuddles and dandles them as Jesus Christ did with the little children:

"And He took them [the children up [h]one by one] in His arms and fervently invoked a] blessing, placing His hands upon them" (Mark 10:16).

When her children fall ill, the church, like a mother, is always ready to nurse them. There are always sick and weak members of the Church's family, not only physically but also spiritually and doctrinally. The family is divinely appointed, just as fully and plainly as any of the others, but it is also a component of both and it is under the jurisdiction of both, as appropriate to each.

True religion does not sever the ties that bind families together. True religion almost never interferes with the hallowed divine institution known as home. It does not cut people apart from their families and turn them into strangers to their own blood. Superstition has separated individuals from their own; a terrible superstition that imposes itself as Christianity has done this. True religion has never done this, though.

The Christians' home is their Eden. This is related, at least in part, to the salvation found in the family. Christians who are joyful spread joy to others. When someone is overflowing with God's blessings, they are able to give more to others. The first place where a Christian has an impact is at home. The family members quickly notice the change when the convert returns home as a changed person. The Christian shares with them what God has wrought. However, even if he or she doesn't, they will quickly realize that something extraordinary has happened to that individual by this or her kindness, love, truth, and holiness. The people around such a person notice a distinct change in the behavior of the converted, their speech, temperament, and countenance. Everyone who is a part of someone who is glorified benefits from the latter's honor.

People spread happiness when their own heart is joyful. America, Ghana or any country is responsible for ensuring the temporal security of her citizens, as well as that of everyone else residing on the land that Providence has entrusted to the care of each individual state. GOD LAID HIS IDEA OF WHAT A NATION SHOULD BE in the camp of the Israelites in the wilderness. If the Israelites had followed God's orders to the letter, the desert would have been a manifestation of the greatest blessing. They would have been a holy people who had gathered around the Holy God's primary temple and were collectively God's servants and priests for His worship.

Israel was a nation in which God's presence sanctified ordinary daily life. God was their leader and forerunner casting a shadow over them during the day in the form of a cloud and providing light at night as a pillar of fire. They were a people who God supported; a people who ate from the bread of heaven; a people who drank from water that sprang from a rock by the power of God; a nation that looked on God as their protector and source of national pride. It would have been extremely well for them if they had been able to carry out the divine commandment. If they had been able to live up to God's expectations allowing the divine plan of love to be fully realized in them, they would have been the happiest sons and daughters of men.

Alas! The Israelites were never satisfied until they got degraded to the level of the majority of mankind; they were constantly striving to resemble the evil nations surrounding them. And we read about the many sorrows of the nation; Israel's experience in the wilderness. Any nation that lives peacefully together with God should be a people to be envied by everyone who knows them. The citizenry of that nation will make God their dwelling place throughout all generations and acquire their resources from Him and move completely at God's command and have a great love for Him.

> *"Superstition has separated individuals from their own;
> a terrible superstition that imposes itself as
> Christianity has done this."*

A City Set On A Hill

Christians are said to be people who are set on a hill, which can mean a number of things, but one of them is that they are not of this world, just as Jesus Christ was not of this world. They are "not of the world, exactly as Jesus was not of the world", rather than merely being outside of it.

"Only be sure as citizens so to conduct yourselves [that] your manner of life [will be] worthy of the good news (the Gospel) of Christ, so that whether I [do] come and see you or am absent, I may hear this of you: that you are standing firm in united spirit and purpose, striving side by side and contending with a single mind for the faith of the glad tidings (the Gospel)" (Philippians 1:27).

This is a crucial distinction since certain individuals are not of the world, yet are not Christians. Among such include sentimentalists, people who unnecessarily sigh and cry all the time and who carry the phrase to the extreme. Their personalities and spirits are so delicate and polished that they are unable to handle everyday tasks. Any involvement with the outside world is regarded as slightly insulting to their spiritual nature.

They often surround themselves with romances and novels; they adore reading books that make them cry; and they always yearn to live in a farmhouse by a wood or to find a secluded cave where they might read books on Solitude indefinitely because they feel "not of the world".

They believe that they are simply too frail to withstand the trials of this evil world. They cannot bear to act like other miserable human beings do because they are so overwhelmingly good. There is a story of a young man who believed he was too spiritually-minded to work. A very wise man advised him thus:

"That is completely true! You are so spiritually minded that you are unable to work; in fact, you are so spiritually minded that you will not be allowed to eat until you work."

That drew him back from his deep spirituality.

Some people milk themselves into a silly sentimentalism. They consume a lot of mind-altering literature and believe that their future is lofty as a result. Those people are undoubtedly "not of the world"; yet, the world does not want them and would not really miss them if they were completely gone forever.

I can state this without using a single needless theological term: A Christian is not of the world in nature just as Jesus Christ was not of the world in nature. Jesus had a divine nature which was flawless, untarnished, and pure. He could not stoop to sin or the things of this world. In another sense, Jesus was human, and the Holy Spirit was the source of His human nature, conceived in the Virgin Mary's womb. His purity prevented anything of a worldly kind from existing within Him. Unlike other men, Jesus was distinct.

The desire to love the world is ingrained in every human being from the moment of birth. Solomon says it well:

"Foolishness is enveloped in a child's heart; but the rod of discipline will drive it far from him." (Proverbs 22:15).

Not only is foolishness present, but it is also entwined with the heart; it is attached to our hearts and it is difficult to break. Every Christian, as it is typical of humanity, had a decidedly earthy and carnal nature before becoming a Christian. Jesus Christ, however, was not. His character was not one of the world. It was fundamentally distinct from everyone else's. He conversed with those from the world, but He was never one of them. Everyone could perceive that Jesus Christ was not of the Pharisee's world even though He often stood side by side with a Pharisee. He had a direct dialogue with the Samaritan woman who sat next to her, but it was obvious that He did not belong in her society and was not a sinner like she was. He socialized with the Publicans, took a seat at their feast, and shared a meal with both Publicans and sinners. Although He interacted with the Publicans, the people could tell by the holy deeds and odd gestures He brought with Him that He was not of their society.

Many people believe that attending church twice a week against those attending church once or not at all makes the difference between being a Christian and being a non-Christian; or taking communion and another not taking it; or reading the bible and the other not reading it; or paying tithes and the other not paying it; or paying attention to holy things and the other paying little attention to them. But any of those does not make one a Christian. The distinction between a Christian and a non-Christian is both external and interior. The distinction is one of nature, not of action. A Christian is essentially different from a worldly person as a dove is from a raven or a lamb from a lion. He or she is not of the world, even in their nature. This is not referring to our corrupt and fallen nature, but rather to our new nature. There is something about a Christian that is completely different from everyone else's.

Nobody could make them worldly. People might do what they like to cause a Christian to fall into some temporary sin, but they cannot make Christian a worldly person. A Christian may backslide, but they cannot become a sinner as they used to be. A Christian is a twice-born human, with the blood of the universe's royal dynasty coursing through their veins. They are a noble people, heaven-born children. A Christian is not of the world in their office. Jesus Christ's office had nothing to do with worldly things.

"Are you then a king?"

"Absolutely, I am a king, but my kingdom does not originate from this world."

"And are you also a priest?"

"Yes, I am a priest, but not in the order of other priest that you know.

"Art thou a leader?"

"Yes, but my policies are not the policies of morality, policies that only concern earthly dealings in parliaments and cabinets and man simply; my policies come down from heaven."

So, we say, Jesus Christ is "not of the world."

Jesus Christ did not hold earthly office and pursued no worldly goals. He did not seek His own applause, fame, or honor; His very office was not of the world. A Christian's office is a priest unto God. Our office is to offer a sacrifice of prayer and praise each day.

A Christian is called unto the office of a priest to be the salt of the earth. They are: "a city set on a hill, a light that cannot be hid". That is the office of a Christian. Our office is not a worldly one. Whether a Christian's office is a minister, a deacon, or a church member, they are not of this world in their office. Even as Jesus Christ was not of the world, our occupation is not worldly. To add but one more, a Christian is not of the world in their character. And that is the chief point in which Jesus Christ was not of the world.

Jesus' character was different from every other man's — pure, perfect, spotless, and such should be the life of a Christian. I do not advocate for sinless behavior in Christians, but I do believe that grace causes people to differ and that God's people will be significantly different from other kinds of people. A servant of God should be a God's person everywhere. As chemists, they cannot not indulge in any tricks whereby people of the world might play with their drugs. As a grocer — if indeed it is not a phantom that such things are done — a Christian could not mix sloe leaves with tea or red lead in the pepper. If they were in any other line of work, a Christian could not, under any circumstances, accept the small shifts known as "business techniques". It is nothing called "business" to a Christian; it is what is known as God's law. They believe they are not from this world. As a result, they violate its styles and dogmas. A heartwarming story about a Christian is told. One day she attended a world congress with people from all walks of life. As she walks to the congress hall, a young girl called out to him, "Ha, there goes a Christian!" The Christian exclaimed: "How do you know I'm a Christian?" The young lady responded: "Because you walk opposite from all the others; that is the way Christians always walk." That is how Christians should constantly walk – in contrast to the world. God's people should not go along with the rest in the latter's worldliness. Their personas should be clearly distinct. Christians should be such that our fellows can recognize us easily and say, "Such a person is a Christian."

AMERICA SET ON A HILL

In 1630, John Winthrop, the father of New England, preached his famous sermon, A Model of Christian Charity. In that message, he likened America to a "…City upon a Hill". The phrase "the city upon a hill" is attributed largely to Winthrop. But people fail to acknowledge that Jesus Christ is the one who first said that during His sermon on the mount "A City that is set on a Hill," Matthew 5:14.

The real content of Winthrop's sermon goes beyond what many people would consider imaginable. In his sermon, Winthrop said:

"For we must consider that we shall be as a city upon a hill; the eyes of all people are upon us. So that if we shall deal falsely with our God in this work we have undertaken, and so cause Him to withdraw His present help from us, we shall be made a story and a byword through the world."

Thus, Winthrop's idea played a vital role in creating the United States as an unmatched, yet, an ideal country of opportunity for the rest of the world. Many politicians have adopted Winthrop's phrase by referring to the United States as "A City that is set on a Hill" to convey a sense of optimism about the country's future.

In his presentation to the General Court of Massachusetts on January 9th, 1961, President-elect, John F. Kennedy repeated the phrase: I have been guided by the standard John Winthrop set before his shipmates on the flagship Arabella (sic) three hundred and thirty-one years ago, as they, too, faced the task of building a new government on a perilous frontier.

"We must always consider that we shall be a city upon a hill; the eyes of all people are upon us."

Ronald Reagan, the 40th president of the United States, depicted a similar picture in the Election Eve Address on November 3, 1980, "A Vision for America." He said:

"I have quoted John Winthrop's words more than once on the campaign trail this year, for I believe that Americans in 1980 are every bit as committed to that vision of a shining 'city on a hill', as were those long-ago settlers. These visitors to that city on the Potomac do not come as white or black, red or yellow; they are not Jews or Christians; conservatives or liberals; or Democrats or Republicans. They are Americans awed by what has gone before, proud of what for them is still ... a shining city on a hill".

John Winthrop's sentiments were not only paraphrased by President Ronald Reagan. But he also made the first sentence of his phrase the cornerstone of his government. Ronald Reagan repeated the same phrases in his final address to the country on January 11, 1989. But in doing so, he articulated his idea of "the shining city upon a hill".

"I've spoken of the shining city all my political life, but I don't know if I ever quite communicated what I saw when I said it. But in my mind, it was a tall, proud city built on rocks stronger than oceans, wind-swept, God-blessed, and teeming with people of all kinds living in harmony and peace; a city with free ports that hummed with commerce and creativity. And if there had to be city walls, the walls had doors, and the doors were open to anyone with the will and the heart to get here. That's how I saw it and see it still".

During his commencement speech at the University of Massachusetts, Boston, on June 2, 2006, the 42nd president, Barack Obama, used John Winthrop's phrase when he said:

"It was right here, in the waters around us, where the American experiment began. As the earliest settlers arrived on the shores of Boston, Salem, and Plymouth, they dreamed of building a City upon a Hill. And the world watched, waiting to see if this improbable idea called America would succeed. More than half of you represent the very first member of your family to ever attend college. In the most diverse university in New England, I look out at a sea of faces that are African American, Hispanic-American, Asian-American, and Arab-American. I see students that have come here from over 100 different countries, believing like those first settlers that they too could find a home in this city on a Hill—that they also could find success in this unlikeliest of places".

During his speech at the 2016 Democratic National Convention, President Barack Obama used the phrase used by President Ronald Reagan to contrast the vision of America with that of then-Republican presidential candidate Donald Trump. Ted Cruz of Texas, a Republican candidate for president in 2016, likewise used John Winthrop's phrase in a speech to announce the end of his presidential bid. 2012 Republican presidential nominee, Mitt Romney, cited John Winthrop's phrase in his 2016 criticism of President Donald Trump's campaign when he said:

"His domestic policies would lead to recession; his foreign policies would make America and the world less safe. He has neither the temperament nor the judgment to be president, and his personal qualities would mean that America would cease to be a shining city on a hill."

In his hearing before the Senate Intelligence Committee in 2017, former FBI Director, James Comey used the phrase:

"We have this big, messy, beautiful country where we fight with each other all the time, but nobody tells us what to think, what to fight about, what to vote for, except other Americans, and that's wonderful

and often painful. But we're talking about a foreign government that tried to shape the way we think, vote, and act. They are going to try to run it down and dirty it up as much as possible. That's what this is about. And they will be back because we remain as difficult as we can be with each other, we continue that shining city on the hill, and they don't like it."

All of their references are quite sincere: "The city upon a Hill", "the shining city upon a hill", A City that is set on a Hill", The sentences that came after the quotes were veritable gold mines; each one was incredibly dense with logic and honesty. It is obvious that one factor contributing to this weight is the burdens that all of these presidents and officials carried. Winthrop appropriately came upon a remark that was a "Flowery quotation". America owes her founding fathers a lot more than she knows.

Many Christians Are Nauseating Unbelievers

I will have to shift my focus from doctrine to practice before I get to this section. I must reprove myself, as do many Christians, for failing to demonstrate sufficiently that we are not of the world in character, just as Jesus Christ was not of the world. Many Christians go to church every day of the week. We assemble around the table at the Lord's Supper; yet, we do not live like Christians. Many people have joined the CHURCH and walked with Christians. However, they are not worthy of the high calling and profession. We Mark the churches worldwide, and our eyes run with tears as to how many people could say that?

"If you belonged to the world, the world would treat you with affection and love you as its own. But because you are not of the world [no longer one with it], but I have chosen (selected) you out of the world, the world hates (detests) you" (John 15:19).

Many Christians are worldly, carnal, and covetous. Nonetheless, they have long been members of churches and stand well with God's people through a hypocritical profession. In the moral universe, identity is far more difficult to make out, for the moral and religious world swarm with pretenders.

It is difficult to know with certainty who among our acquaintances is a Christian and who is not.

Deception is so easy and is nowadays practiced in so masterly a manner that I wot it is difficult to know a son of God from a son of Belial. You may sit down and commune with someone wearing a clerical, and find out that he or she is a Judas. You may walk side by side with one who seems to be a Simon Peter and they prove themselves to be a Simon Magus. What is worse, Christians may be deceived about themselves, and whereas one may have thought their body to be a temple of the Holy Ghost, they may suddenly discover it to have been made a den of all forms of evilness. If God sends all the angels to the world to separate the righteous from the wicked, I wonder if he will be able to distinguish the difference. It is fearful that it might puzzle Angel Gabriel Himself to tell whether some Christians are indeed who they profess to be. Yet, this is a very important matter, for many Christians are not right and cannot clear their consciences that they are right. They, thus, live in a state of perpetual unrest, never at any moment possessing safety.

We ought to know — we should never be at peace till we do know — whether we are the children of God or not, and since the outward aspect so often deceives, visible signs are not to be relied upon. It becomes imperative upon us that we search deep and look for signs that will not deceive us prying into the very core and marrow of our being until we have resolved the weighty question of whether we are the children of God or the heirs of wrath. These days, when worldly religions are so similar, it is exceedingly difficult to tell them apart.

However, God is not susceptible to human deception. They might be able to outwit others — including themselves — with their impressive titles and credentials, but not God. A father may be able to use a unique identifier that only she is privy to instantly recognize her child. The impostor may have a voice that sounds like Jacob's, hands that aren't too dissimilar from Jacob's, and the ability to recall a lot of details about his youth that seem to be known only by the real child. But the father remembers that there was a secret spot, and if it's not there, he dismisses the pretender; if he finds that personal sign, he will recognize the alleged child as his own.

"In the moral universe, identity is far more difficult to make out, for the moral and religious world swarm with pretenders."

Backsliding Before Excommunication

Walking in the light as Jesus Christ is in the light and thus having fellowship with Him is the proper condition for a child of God. Our only safe standing is to abide in Him and have His words and Himself abide in us. But too often, we follow afar off; we live in a very limited and remote fellowship with Jesus Christ. It is a stunning fact that we are ignorant of the wickedness of our own hearts. Like Hazael, we do not believe that we are as bad enough to do any of the things we sometimes anticipate. So, like Hazael we ask:

"…What is your servant, only a dog, that he should do this monstrous thing? (2 Kings 8:13).

We are conscious enough that our heart is not so pure, but it might consent to do many evil things. Yet, crimes so flagrant as we are called to answer or are foretold of, we think ourselves quite incapable of committing. Very often, many tyrants could not believe that such wanton cruelty lurked in their breasts or those barbarities towards women and children at war could be perpetrated with their sanction. The fact is, unless we are changed and aided by divine grace, we often refuse to pay our great God the service due to Him.

Backsliding Christians make many great mistakes. At first, people prioritize their temporal mercies in their hearts. Because their business prospers, they do not consider that their soul is perishing. They forget their spirit is hungry for heaven's food since there is enough on the table for themselves and their children. The regressive thinks so much about a world where we only stay for a few awful years that they ignore the world where they must live forever. Such ignorance is especially repugnant in someone who was previously a professing Christian since they knew or pretended to know something about the eternal's superiority over the temporal, the futility of things earthly and the glory of things heavenly.

They prioritized the shadows of time over the realities of eternity. They say, "We have to live," but they forget that they will die. They forget the cataract scarlet with the blood of souls adown whose huge steeps those treacherous waves would soon drive them down as long as the stream glides smoothly and the lovely flow of the river of their delight is undisturbed. It is a grave error for anyone to place so much value on this wretched body of clay while overlooking the beautiful treasure of the immortal soul.

Yet, because things go well with the backsliding — because their spouses are in health, their children blooming, their house well furnished, their property increasing, they say:

"...Soul, you have many good things laid up, [enough] for many years. Take your ease; eat, drink, and enjoy yourself merrily" (Luke 12:19).

They do not disturb themselves though heaven is black with lowering tempest, and the light of God's countenance is hidden from them. A backslider thinks the loss of God's presence to be a trifle because they are succeeding in the world as though they should count it nothing to lose their life if they may but keep their raiment whole to be buried in. One error led to another; hence, a backslider holds their temporal things upon a wrong tenure. Alas! Backsliding is among God's people very common. Sin abounds so that none can measure its heinousness or power, but grace does much more abound where sin abounds. Sin is like a dragon pouring torrents from its mouth, while God's mercy is like a raging ocean with no shores.

Throughout the Scriptures, there is a fierce competition between man's sin and God's grace, with each striving to be more plentiful than the other. Under the legal dispensation, anyone with leprosy or any contagious disease was put without the camp. It is true that sin is a dreadful disease that has attacked the whole human race. It came to this earth when that old serpent, the devil, tempted Mother Eve. Then did this dire disease begin to course through human veins, and it has descended to everyone in the race. And at this moment, it lurks within each one of us. It is worse than lurking, for it has manifested itself and displayed its venom and virulence. Sin has shown itself in life, and, like leprosy upon the brow of the man suffering from that dreadful disease, it is visible upon us all.

The disease of sin is exceedingly injurious. Like diseases that affect the heart, sin has turned the heart of Mankind into a stone. Like diseases that afflict the eyes and the ears, sin has blinded and blocked mankind's understanding — our mental and spiritual eyesight. Like some diseases that affect the hands, and, in our natural condition, we cannot work for God's glory, or grasp gospel blessings because the disease of sin has withered our hands spiritually. But I would not linger on that word because there is a word of comfort to consider. Because of Jesus Christ, God does not instantly banish a backslider right at the moment when they sin. Such lamentations may end when the backslider's heart grows tender. If they see sin sufficiently to make them bewail it, they may then look away from it, for God says: "I will heal their backsliding." There is solace in the fact that God here depicts the heinous sin of backsliding in the form of an illness. He does not say: "I will pardon their backsliding." The term does cover this, but "I will heal" it.

Many are the voices around a backslider and within them which persuade them to render unto the great Householder His due. God always sends many messengers to them. They hear the Word of God and the record of the testimonies of His inspired messengers, and those virtually speak to the backsliding Christian. Besides that, backsliders are always surrounded by people of God and encompassed by other Christians who have appealed to them on God's behalf.

They have been called to God by the most earnest entreaties of faithful men and affectionate women. Discourses have been addressed to them, which might have moved hearts of stone. And though stirred for the moment, they remain obstinate enemies to God, dishonest to His claims, careful of this world, and forgetful of the world to come. The messengers of God are urged to speak by the love of their hearts, and they have tried to bring backsliders to repent of rebellion and to yield themselves at once to God. But in many cases, none of those have been successful. Everyone should appreciate a messenger who comes to us after being rejected repeatedly and just doing so out of love for us.

Loving Admonition

Concerning the backslider, every Christian, priest, or office is sent to reconcile the former to God, the Father. We are to warn the backslider.

"I tell you, No; but unless you repent (change your mind for the better and heartily amend your ways, with abhorrence of your past sins), you will all likewise perish and be lost eternally." (Luke 13:5).

A priest or all others are to set the way of reconciliation before a backslider and bids them believe in Jesus Christ and live. With many a charming parable, we are to draw the far-off prodigal home to the bosom of forgiving love. The very coming of Jesus Christ, the Son of God in human form, as Emmanuel, God with us, is love's great plea for reconciliation.

Who can resist so powerful an argument? It is in the person of Jesus Christ that God makes His last and strongest appeal to the human conscience. By Jesus Christ of God, the priest and the officers virtually say to the backslider, "Turn ye, turn ye: why will ye die, O house of Israel?" And I would to God that the answer might be from many a heart:

"Come and let us return to the Lord, for He has torn so that He may heal us; He has stricken so that He may bind us up! (Hosea 6:1).

A priest intends to be exceedingly gentle in all their sermons they preach to the backslider. They have to water minds as tender herbs and water them in the same fashion as the small rain does. A priest should not be a beating hail or a down-pouring shower, but they have to be "as the small rain upon the tender herb"

Discipline in the church, suspension, and excommunication are mostly doctrinal action. So, when a priest speaks to a backslider, they should say, "My doctrine shall drop as the rain." Other times, their doctrinal sermon may have seemed to be most appropriately preached with clenched fists. The very idea of a doctrinal sermon seemed to mean a fight, a sort of spiritual duel, in which the priest was evidently bent upon demolishing somebody or another who held contrary views. The priest should never let doctrine distill as rain and drop as dew, "as the small rain upon the tender herb."

At certain turning points of the road, they must contend earnestly for the faith once delivered to the saints. But they are to recollect that their contentions are the contentions of love and that it ill becomes the Christian who holds the truth of a loving Jesus to hold it in bitterness or contends for it with rancor. Many priests have been guilty in this matter. However, some have felt no bitterness; and when they have spoken forcibly, they have yet restrained themselves from harder things that any true Christian might truthfully have brought forth.

Sadly, many priests have been forced into controversy for which they have no taste and no pleasure. They have been driven into it: they have never sought it. To spread the gospel, they should choose the gentler method: it is only to defend it that they have to draw the sword. Priests, as well as every Christian, should fight for the truth. They should be willing to live or die for the truth. But if they wish to spread it, they will do it best by letting it drop as rain and distill as the dew, gently and tenderly, "as the small rain upon the tender herb."

It is equally remarkable that the discourse of a priest and a backslider should be a sermon of rebuke. He is to rebuke the backslider and rebuke them, too, with no small degree of sternness.

"But Jeshurun (Israel) grew fat and kicked. You became fat, you grew thick, you were gorged and sleek! Then he forsook God Who made him and forsook and despised the Rock of his salvation." (Deuteronomy 32:15).

A priest is to warn the backslider of their great sin, and they should not hesitate to say: *"They are a nation void of counsel; neither is there any understanding in them."* Yet, the priest should make sure they rebuke with the utmost meekness and still be as the soft dew and gentle rain. His or her upbraiding must be done in tenderness. Rebukes given in an unkind spirit had better not be given at all.

The priest should not address a backsliding Christian in the most terrific strains. He should cease telling them: "The Lord is coming! The Lord is coming! You will be all destroyed!" That way of speaking to a backslider is plenty of sounds, though I fear not an excess of sense. It is a savor of delirious prophecy that goes beyond the Scriptures into personal visions and figments of the man's brain. I wonder what such a priest would hope to do. A priest who speaks to a backslider in that tone will find backsliders who take in everything a priest says as a curious display. Perhaps, they had better rage like a sea in a storm than give the people no warning. Yet, I do not suppose any good could come of the shouting.

On the other hand, if a priest speaks gently to a backslider, one by one, concerning faith in God; and the great love of Jesus Christ, perhaps, there would be great results. One would not look for good fruit from the boisterous shouting of nonsense; yet, many priests feel that if they shout and perspire on backsliders, something must be affected. Wisdom does not learn her exercises among the athletes but among calm scholars. We do not use black people's eyes to make them see, bully them into peace, or kick them into heaven. To strive, cry, lift up, and cause clamorous voices to be heard in the streets is not Jesus Christ's way. Not a syllable have I to say against zeal, even when it breaks over all bounds of propriety. But it is the zeal that God values, not the outbursts.

Even worldly people question greatly whether too often physical force is not mistaken for spiritual power. And it is an error of a mischievous kind. If they can, a priest and church officials should draw backsliders with bands of love, not with cart ropes, and with "cords of a man", not such cords as they put about dogs and bulls.

There must be in all rebukes an abounding gentleness, softness, and holy sorrow. When Paul is writing a very strong condemnation, he says:

"I now tell you even weeping, that they are the enemies of the cross of Christ." (Phil 3:18).

Jesus Christ denounces the doom of Jerusalem, but it is with a flood of tears. He cries: "Woe unto thee, Chorazin!" but He feels some woe within His own soul while He is uttering woe to them. I pray that with every church discipline that is a doctrinal discourse, it will be tender, and though it is a rebuking discourse, it will still be "as the small rain upon the tender herb."

Degrading Officials

The puritan idea of a church that is completely simple is a myth. However, it is necessary to purge the Church's membership, particularly her officers, of blatant and well-known offenders in order to restore her purity. Reprimanding offenders is appropriate, even for their own benefit.

A true church is built on eternal truth. An ancient Latin proverb states that the truth must win since it is powerful. The truth is and will always be. It is the only thing with substance and must endure the passage of time.

For many years, the Church held that all ecclesiastical court procedures were in the defendant's favor. The English ecclesiastical courts have kept the memory of this theory because their charges against a person were, and likely still are, declared to be for the good of his or her soul, *pro saute anitne sue.*

The Church is a well-established, a ruling institution. She has Pastors who serve as her executive officers, and it is their duty to guide and care for the congregation. As part of this job, they are also expected to serve as role models for the congregation. The Church takes special care of the faith and morals of her members, enacting special rules regarding them everywhere. Before being appointed to office, every pastor and official would have their moral and religious character examined, and if they were lacking, they would be degraded or removed.

They are only appropriately removed following a judicial investigation. As a result, two different types of church discipline exist - clerical discipline and lay discipline. In terms of lay discipline, excommunication (ultimunm supplicium) is the ultimate sanction, whilst, for clerical degradation, ecclesiastical law refers to the rules that the Church has established for the application of those two types of punishment. As long as church discipline is only enforced through the suspension and degradation of delinquent priests and the suspension or excommunication of offending laymen, there can be no realistic basis for America, Ghana or other nations to protest and no risk of conflict. The State can only see the Church as a voluntary society with excommunication representing a person's exclusion from that society and degradation being the removal of a member of its executives. The only thing the State can do is agree to the exclusions and removals. If the crimes like rape or theft that caused their removal also break her laws, she is still free to punish them. If the exclusion or removal directly affects civil or material rights, she may dispute whether the ecclesiastical proceedings have been performed in accordance with church law in her civil courts. The State can hardly be denied this much, and she makes no further demands in many nations. There can be no collision if those principles are applied on both sides.

The historical partnerships between the Church and the State, in which each granted the other a share of their respective power, gave rise to the old conflicts. Each further asserted that they had exclusive jurisdiction over certain individuals whom it believed should be exempt from the other's authority. In some circumstances, the State even granted the Church authority over certain matters. The Church, for her part, gave the State a sizable portion of the authority to choose her (the State) top officials.

The obvious distinctions between the two jurisdictions — marked by the distinct goals of the two institutions and their various means of upholding their authority — were lost. People's opinions on the matter got muddled, and their passions and interests roused them against one another. The ecclesiastical history of Europe throughout many centuries is mostly a record of conflict with the State. This situation was made worse by the idea that the two societies were the same. It was assumed that one of the two groups in charge of a society must be better than the other.

The issue of who was superior must come up. Both had taken on a federative structure, each comprising smaller federations with their own heads. Those were all subordinate to the head of some greater federation, and eventually, all were subordinate to the head of one vast federation, of which they were all members. The largest and most powerful federation regarding moral and intellectual power was and still is the Church.

In terms of physical power, the State was superior. As a result, intellectual and physical power has been in conflict for a long time. The Pope was in charge of the unified Church of Western Europe. All of the clergy recognized his authority, and they were powerful everywhere. The largest State federation wasn't even close to being that big. Since the Pope was able to command the military might that the Church lacked and should not have by playing off one temporal prince against another, every temporal prince in Europe thought that it was in his best advantage to be friendly with the Pope. This gave the Pope the confidence to assert his superiority over the leaders of the States. The assertion was contested everywhere, and it led to several conflicts between the Church and the State.

Thankfully, that was one of the collision causes that stopped in many countries along with all the others that were identified. The Reformation was profoundly influenced by the struggle for ascendancy which decided it in the State's favor. The power of the Pope was revoked in areas where the Reformation was successful. Without a defender outside the State's borders, the local clergy was fully subsumed under her control.

His power was, nevertheless, significantly curtailed, and that of the temporal sovereigns advanced in those nations that did not renounce their allegiance to the Pope. The State is now the main proponent of the Church's independence, as well as the main opponent of the union of Church and State. In America, there has been a long-standing growing antagonism toward the union - enjoyable sensation, albeit one that isn't truly grounded in reality. Many significant negative outcomes of the union have benefited the Church more than the State or particular individuals. Popery is merely a backlash against it. Once upon a time, the Church had a voluntary financial system that was based on the concept of obligation.

In exchange for agreeing to rely solely on her endowments gleaned from State assistance, the Church agreed to the formation of a partnership between herself and the State. Soon after ceasing to provide any assistance, the State` falsely claimed to be the source of the donations. It was necessary to go back to the voluntary system because the Church's needs outgrew its endowments. However, the previous way of doing business had been lost, and people just had a sense of responsibility and a habit of giving. That is why many Churches are poor. People in many different countries allegedly despise the union of Church and State. What they fear most is the Church's tyranny over the State and over themselves, yet neither of which poses any threat.

A great and unmixed evil, without a doubt, has resulted from the union in many nations where the State now dominates the Church. Many Africans once looked to the State to protect them from the priest. The State was on the side of religion. There are some people who appear to be doing the same thing now, but there is cause for concern that there may be too many of them who see the State as the defender of religious liberalism.

Many Africans claim to have a close bond with the Church despite strongly opposing the idea of an autonomous ecclesiastical authority. However, many genuinely support the current system since they see it as merely a product of the State. Because of the English-speaking Europeans who immigrated to Africa, many Africans retain strong hostility toward the Church which encompasses any organization of religion that imposes power. They claim to strongly oppose any association between the Church and the State. However, a latent desire exists to hold the Church accountable to the public and the broader society.

The effects of this sensation can be seen. The so-called organs of public opinion, the secular newspapers, enjoy interfering in religious affairs and holding them to a different standard. Some religious organizations and church publications have a penchant for appealing to public opinion because they themselves are influenced by it. Such appeals, as well as those who make them, are often well-liked outside of the Church.

Often known as the general public, society is always prepared to side with the State against the Church. Society is far more willing to impose its ideas on the Church and set its rules, just as it mostly does with the State. She actually favors the State because the general public understands and values temporal interests more than spiritual ones. The State has a greater concrete authority than the Church since the latter can also enforce her laws through temporal punishments.

Only those who have faith can feel the Church's decrees since her authority is spiritual. The vast majority of people dismiss it because they see it as simply tyranny. The Church is also suspected of attempting to impose a moral code that is stricter than societies or the law of the United States of America. The Church is, therefore, unpopular with the general public (Society).

The Church may be very cautious in preventing conflicts with society or with the such as America, Ghana or any other country, but it would be really irresponsible for her to cause a conflict with either if it could be avoided. Many Church members are susceptible to being mobilized by the State or the society against her.

But occasionally, the Church might have to acknowledge a difference of opinion. Most people are unstable in their friendships; they meet someone one day and want to be as nice as possible with them; the next day, they run into them; they have no idea what the new friend may have done to anger them, but they turned away. Some people even go a step further and incorporate their instability into their moral character.

They are a peculiar breed of Christians I will not dispute of. Because of their broad consciences, which allow them to accept many actions that tender-hearted people would consider immoral, even though they act morally in the majority of their actions, these people will occasionally strain the boundaries of godliness. However, a devout Christian will usually say, "Dear me! What a tragic shame to the cause of Christianity so-and-so is.

The Church would do better without them because they dishonor the name of Jesus Christ in such a way. Yet, the church might not identify any transgressions to use as justification for excommunicating them.

THE SUSPENDED IN A MARVELLOUS COMMUNITY

It is fairly amazing that many self-righteous Christians who appear to value the law of Moses are often completely unaware of what is the fundamental essence and spirit of that rule.

"Bear (endure, carry) one another's burdens and [a]troublesome moral faults, and in this way fulfill and observe perfectly the law of Christ (the Messiah) and complete [b]what is lacking [in your obedience to it]." (Galatians 6:2).

They are so upright that they become severe and harsh and censorious, which is unrighteous, because even the law's righteousness is the righteousness of love, "because all the law is fulfilled in one word," that is, "love". Such Christians are, as far as they could, putting themselves again under the old ceremonial law. They forsook the gospel way of justification by faith and sought to be made perfect by their personal obedience to the law.

Many Christians execute the sternness and severity of the law in their relationships with others and with themselves. However, there is none of the kindness, gentleness, sweetness, or graciousness that even the law itself demanded when it declared:

"And He replied to him, you shall love the Lord your God with all your heart and with all your soul and with all your mind (intellect). This is the great (most important, principal) and first commandment. And a second is like it: You shall love your neighbor as [you do] yourself" (Matthew 22:37-39).

God does not tell any Christian to spy out their neighbors' faults. The connection of "Bear ye one another's burden" shows that the word "burdens" in the context means "Moral faults". To a godly person, a fault is a burden. The worst burden they have to carry is that they are not perfect; that is what troubles them. They do not despise those with heavy burdens to bear, thus people who have been suspended due to their faults.

If a Christian is found with an open sin and they are suspended, a godly Christian does not say, "Oh!" "There is that sister who fornicated and was suspended." They do not think little of a suspended Christian and look at them as poor souls they have been. A godly Christian does not despise the afflicted, especially the mentally, desponding, and sorrowful among God's people. They do not turn aside and say: "I can't stand talking to people like them; they have such a sad demeanor and character." But they joined hearts with the apostle, Paul, and "Bear you one another's burdens".

They do not run away from other people because they see that they are burdened. A Christian does not say:

"I like to be with the cheerful, I cannot go and spend my life comforting the mourners."

A mind such as that was not in Jesus Christ, who "a bruised reed He will not break, and a dimly burning wick He will not quench; He will bring forth justice in truth" (Isaiah 42:3).

Every Christian must be taught to sympathize with the imprisoned and grieving! Without a doubt, having fellowship with those who, through their own sins, have greatly afflicted my mind will drag our own spirits down. However, we must be willing to be dragged down; it will benefit us. However, we must be willing to be dragged down; it will benefit us.

When God will surely bless us if we are ready to stoop to the very least of His people whom Satan has sought to steal, kill, and destroy. You might be able to stand up to Goliath like young David, for such an action is grand and heroic. But to look after the poor little lambs of the flock which scarcely seem they are alive is quite another matter.

Yet, that is what God wants us to do: "Bear ye one another's burdens." Carry the lambs in your bosom, and be compassionate to those who are affected by imprisonment or anything else. Let us be as our Lord Jesus Christ was. He was of a gentle, a loving spirit, seeking to bear the infirmities of the weak. Let every Christian, especially those who are strong, be careful not to be like those fat cattle described in the prophecy of Ezekiel. They pushed the sickly herd with their horns and pushed the skinny cattle with their sides and shoulders. If we do that, God will order us to be taken to the slaughterhouse, for that is a lot of the fed beasts that are so big and brutal. The air uproots the lofty tree, barely bending the lower willow. Blessed are the Christians who never exalt themselves over the suspended, the weak, and the afflicted among the children of God.

Excommunications

Excommunication is a humiliating word. The sound of it ought to arouse the spirit of a backslider, and the consciousness of having been associated with it should make every Christian lay their mouths in the dust. Only God, of all beings, has absolute stability; He is devoid of change or even the slightest indication of turning.

"Every good gift and every perfect (free, large, full) gift is from above; it comes down from the Father of all [that gives] light, in [the shining of] Whom there can be no variation [rising or setting] or shadow cast by His turning [as in an eclipse]" (James 1:17).

Since Adam's fall, the world no longer exhibits perfect stability. He was stable enough while in the garden following his master's orders, but after eating the forbidden fruit, he slipped and caused all of his descendants' standing positions to tremble. Let me, thus, address myself and all Christians. Our first Adam spoiled us all, and while the second Adam has regenerated us, He has not yet healed the flaws that the first Adam bequeathed to us as a somber legacy. None of us are as stable as we ought to be. Even the most capable members of humanity are subject to change, making them unstable and less effective.

Yet, it is remarkable that even though we have lost absolute stability, we still appreciate it. Perhaps, there is no virtue, or better still, no collection of virtues, that the world values more than mental and behavioral stability.

Rarely have people ever referred to a man as outstanding who lacked consistency and mental fortitude to stand by their convictions. I have no idea why, but once someone is strong and consistent, we always look up to them. Consistency had led people to falsely laud those with moral standards far below what was necessary and describe them as wonderful when they were not. Even when we are certain that someone is wrong, we admire them for their resilience.

In Ghana, West Africa, a crazy woman used to come up with an absurd story that we could only laugh at her. We disagreed with her concept and despised it, but she persisted, and we used to say: "Well, there is nothing like a person standing beside their conviction," As she persevered in fruitless attempts to fulfill her dream, we saw her tenaciously believing that her plan would ultimately succeed. We even admired the insane who lacked intelligence and common sense.

How unstable many Christians are! A subset of people claim to be Christians, yet they are Christians of a particular kind. I am not being so severe as to condemn anyone, but I must denounce the fault I'm about to point out. There are Christians in so many churches in the Christian world that are unstable as water!

"But unstable and boiling over like water, you shall [c]not excel and have the preeminence [of the firstborn], because you went to your father's bed; you defiled it—he went to my couch!" (Genesis 49:4).

They are regular congregants; they have been baptized in water, they partake in the Lord's Supper, they attend prayer meetings, church meetings, and everything else associated with the Christian community with which they are associated. They are never behindhand in religious performances. They are the most devout hypocrites, the most pious formalists that could be discovered, and range the wide world o'er.

On Sundays, their faith is of the highest caliber. When they are in their pews, their godliness is unparalleled. They sing the most beautiful praise. They pray the longest and most insincere prayer imaginable. They tithe anise, mint, and cummin; they fast twice a week; or if they do not fast, they are just as holy and righteous in not fasting as if they did. They are perfectly acceptable from every religious standpoint. The only problem is that there is nothing to be desired in terms of the externals of godliness.

They have a strong attachment to anything holy and devoted, but sadly,! In the worst sense, these people are as fragile as water. They bring disgrace to the cause for which they advocate: not even the vilest profane swearer causes more disrespect to God's holy name than they do, and it is difficult to explain the situation.

One way in which sinners frequently excuse themselves is by endeavoring to get some apology for their own iniquities from the inconsistencies of Christians. That is one of the reasons why there are many sins in the world. A true Christian should have been a rebuke to the sinner. Wherever they go, they should have been a living protest against the evil of sin. The worldly person should not have found any grounds to have slandered a Christian but to have said:

"There was a man in the land of Uz whose name was Job, and that man was blameless and upright, and one who [reverently] feared God and abstained from and shunned evil [because it was wrong" (Job 1:1).

Alas, alas! However, sinners have not always used calumny and lies. It is too true that many professing Christians have given a real bona fide cause to the world for excusing themselves in their sin: the inconsistencies of professors, the want of heart in piety, and the absence of devout earnestness have given sad grounds to the ungodly to justify themselves in their sin.

"If we say we have no sin [refusing to admit that we are sinners], we delude and lead ourselves astray, and the Truth [which the Gospel presents] is not in us [does not dwell in our hearts]" (1 John 1:8).

The Church used her divine authority to expel such persistently disobedient Christians. Such action is not done to downplay the awful weight of the phrases that support the excommunication power. Excommunication, however, is nothing more to those without faith than being barred from church membership and receiving church benefits, whether or not they are formally affiliated with the Church. To them, this only entails banishment from a mutually beneficial community. Excommunication is a last recourse, just as death is the state's ultimate punishment. It is the *ultimun supplicium.*

Jesus Christ gave the Church the authority of excommunication in these words:

"[Now having received the Holy Spirit and being [b]led and directed by Him] if you forgive the sins of anyone, they are forgiven; if you retain the sins of anyone, they are retained." (John 20:23).

The Church's responsibility is to keep an eye out for souls, and in another source, this is explicitly stated as the basis for her authority.

"Obey your spiritual leaders and submit to them [continually recognizing their authority over you], for they are constantly keeping watch over your souls and guarding your spiritual welfare, as men who will have to render an account [of their trust]. [Do your part to] let them do this with gladness and not with sighing and groaning, for that would not be profitable to you [either]" (Hebrews 13:17).

The Excommunicated In The Visible Church

Apostle Paul warns us of certain unchristian characters who will appear in the last times. Though we have seen a number of those in the past times, his warning leads us to believe that they will appear in more numbers in the last days than in any other age. Indeed, it is a very terrible list as mentioned by Apostle Paul.

"Lovers of their own selves, covetous, boasters, proud, blasphemers, disobedient to parents, unthankful, unholy, without natural affection, trucebreakers, false accusers, incontinent, fierce, despisers of those that are good, traitors, heady, high-minded, lovers of pleasures more than lovers of God." (2 Timothy 3:3-4).

Those will swarm like flies as the year progresses, and that will make the times ahead extremely dangerous. We are currently approaching that point in time. Clearly, some of those people are within the church, and that makes it the most difficult aspect of the last days experience. However, the Holy Spirit shall surely find them out because of their deeds and fruits. Those will certainly betray their pretentious worship in the church as stated by the following scripture.

"Having a form of godliness, but denying the power thereof…" (2 Timothy 3:5a).

All such characters on the list, in their consistency, may be led to excommunication from the church. And God, through Paul, warns His children thus:

"…Avoid [all] such people [turn away from them]" (2 Timothy 3:5b).

It is possible to be moral while breaching men's rules. Rebellion against the traditions of a man-made church may be evidence of enlightenment. To refuse homage to a proud hierarchy may be a bounden duty. All who claim the right to manhood must reject the bonds of custom, the shackles of fashion, and the manacles of priestcraft. Of course, it is not a sin to sever them.

Sin is a lack of conformity to God's will; sin is disobedience to God's order; sin is a neglect of the obligations of the creature-Creator relationship; Injustice to my fellow-creature is truly evil, but its essence is that it is a sin against God who created the relationship that I have violated. That is the essence.

The guilt lies in all excommunicated offenders in their disobedience to the good God who has a claim to be served by them with all their heart, soul, and strength. They are never moved to perform virtue by the thought that God will approve of it. They have no conscience for repentance even if the table is laden with the abundance of His providence; they have no remorse for a change of heart despite the fact that the sick chamber is made to feel the dread of His rod; they have no desire to turn to God despite the fact that they wander through all the fields of nature and see evidence of Deity on every side; they have no conscience to perceive God's hand in every incident of their life.

In this regard, they, unfortunately, live like brutes! Many of them die in the same way, without God, without the church and her followers, and without hope - earth scavengers may bury them in the earth.

Spiritual Excommunication From The Invisible Church

Sin is the world's greatest problem — not death, illness, famine, poverty, hatred, etc. From SIN, everything else follows naturally.

From the SIN wellspring of resentment and malice, all kinds of misery draw their bitterness. Sin may convert every good thing into a bad thing, change love into hatred, turn wealth into poverty, turn friends into enemies, and turn life into death. Without the poisoned darts of sin, Satan would not have been capable of hurting Adam and Eve or anyone else.

What is worse is that SIN is deceitful, and Christians need to take seriously the idea that sin is deceitful because here is where our biggest threat is. If sin comes to a Christian as sin, by God's grace, they will be quick to hate it and strong in repelling it. A Christian immediately avoids a behavior once they are aware that it is against God's law. When something is clearly evil, it is easy for even an unbeliever to avoid it.

If sin were to announce itself, "I am Sin", with a loud trumpet and a large banner, that would be good. Then, every Christian would be aware of and realize the danger in every circumstance.

But sin's deceitfulness is especially destructive. It dons a lovely outfit and approaches Christians using a different love language than its own. Therefore, even devout Christians who abstain from sin may gradually succumb to temptation and deception.

The most miserable sinners in the world are those who call themselves Christians but consistently engage in secret sin. A truly wicked unbeliever who brazenly goes for walks while proclaiming:

"I am a fornicator; I am not ashamed of it", will experience utter misery in the next world, but they will still enjoy their moment of pleasure.

An unbelieving accountant who steals billions of dollars and confesses to being an evil man while cursing and swearing when caught has, at least, some peace in their mind. But what a horrible living it must be for the Christian who walks with God's minister, connected with God's Church, appears before God's people and unites with them and then lives in sin! It must be a very solemn thing for every Christian to remember that God is constantly looking from heaven.

A good man is quick to notice other good people just as those who are wise can pick up wisdom fast from those who are wise. When the Godly God looks down from heaven, He can quickly tell if a Christian is godly. But even while we may be sure that God's description of people on earth, including many Christians, is not unkind or unfair, it is not at all like what I have heard flattering loved ones say about them. He says:

"No one understands [no one intelligently discerns or comprehends; no one seeks out God." (Romans 3:11).

There is not one who does good; they have all been pushed out of the way and have collectively lost their value. The world we live in has made it fashionable to talk about "the dignity of manhood" and "the majesty of manhood." However, that is how God perceived the man in our natural State, and He knows the truth about us better than we do. God doesn't commit injustice or exaggeration. He has no desire to exacerbate the already dire State of humanity. He provides outlines of absolute truthfulness for our photographs. The light of God is the light of truth, and what He shows us is unquestionably exactly as He portrays it.

When God speaks about men, there is a sense of unity throughout all of humanity. He employs those enormous all-encompassing "alls" to characterize the entire race without exception. We are all out of the way, and as a collective, we are no longer profitable. In order to prevent anyone from escaping, the Omniscient God utilizes both positive and negative language: "There is none that doeth good, no, not one." On a Sunday morning, a young, devout Christian lady asked me:

"Aunty, why is it that not all Christians receive the same punishment when they sin?" And why do some avoid punishment? I replied: *"Surely, not every Christian experience will be the same."*

Yes, many self-proclaimed Christians live by dubious moral standards but never suffer the consequences. Many Christians have hearts that are just as corrupt as those who have polluted themselves with external immorality. Because they are not as severely tempted as the others and are not subject to the same conditions as those who are disciplined, such Christians appear to escape penalty and open excommunication. They may believe they are significantly better than those whose sins have been discovered and who have been excommunicated because they have kept theirs secret. But if they had been exposed like the excommunicated, if the devil had abandoned them as others have been, they would have turned into something just as repulsive as they. If it had not been for God's grace, many Christians would have fallen into the one kind of sin that everyone despises.

Many Christians commit what they refer to as "little sins," which are equally awful and disgusting in God's eyes but not so common that people notice them "…Is it not a little one?" (Genesis 19:20). We usually hold the sin that does mankind the most harm to be the worst one. Therefore, if you label someone a criminal, their blood will immediately boil. They won't allow you to refer to them in such a way. However, a criminal is someone who has caused harm to another person. In that situation, a criminal would prefer to be called a sinner and to which they would respond, "Oh, yes! Everyone born of a woman is an all-sinner". They see being called a sinner as only an offender against God. Thus they do not see it as being at all significant.

When human being offends their fellow humans, our conscience instantly informs us of the fact that we are acting improperly. But when we wrong God, moral sense harshly reprimands us! If a Christian were ungrateful to another Christian or friends, they should feel that they had done a grievous wrong. A Christian might view it as a serious offense if they were to be disloyal to their nation and rebel against her laws.

But even when many Christians continue to disobey God and the best laws ever made, their shame does not reach the depths that a proper sense of wrong would. They are not horrified by their spiritual treason! Some Christians' behaviors demonstrate how human nature has been corrupted and how our judgment has become distorted. Otherwise, we would immediately believe that dishonoring the Creator of all the universe is a far worse crime than wronging our fellow humans.

Committed Christians will never lose their fear of God because of little sins. They will accept the most horrendous suffering in exchange for even the smallest deviation from the path of truth and morality. They are aware that small actions can have large effects and that even minor sins can violate important moral rules.

My main goal is to demonstrate the mercy and compassion of our God in sending Jesus Christ to earth as a ransom for a world that is lost and dying

"For God so loved the world, that he gave His only begotten Son, that whosoever believeth in him should not perish, but have everlasting love." (John 3:16).

Therefore, I extend an invitation to anyone who is the greatest sinner like myself as He will not turn away anybody who comes to Him but will, without a doubt, give them eternal life.

"All whom My Father gives (entrusts) to Me will come to Me; and the one who comes to Me I will most certainly not cast out [I will never, no never, reject one of them who comes to Me]." (John 6:37).

However, I must point out that if someone wants to be evil, they should adopt the lifestyle of a roistering sinner who engages in open sin. But if someone claims to be a Christian, they shouldn't behave dishonestly, or be a coward, or sin secretly. They should not claim to be God's and live their lives for the devil.

Every sincere sinner will be ashamed of such a lifestyle since it is cheating the devil. Such abominable hypocrisy is one thing that has strangled the Church and severed her own sinews in two. Many godly souls have fallen victim to people who claim to be Christians but are not. By falling into the trap and being taken in by those hypocritical Christians, such kind hearts have been destroyed. With everything I have said, I've come precariously close to saying that God could be unable to pardon a secret Christian sinner who falsely claimed to be someone they are not.

He may pardon the sinner who riots publicly and doesn't claim to be better. However, God hates the person who fawns, cants, pretends, prays, and then continues to live in sin. He abhors them fervently and excommunicates them from the invisible Church because He cannot stand them.

"So, because you are lukewarm and neither cold nor hot, I will spew you out of My mouth!" (Revelation 3:16).

Those who God excommunicates from the invisible Church but yet partake in the visible Church's fellowship must face punishment. They are said to have fallen into the hands of the living God.

"It is a fearful (formidable and terrible) thing to incur the divine penalties and be cast into the hands of the living God!" (Hebrews 10: 31).

I have heard people talk of someone falling into the devil's hands. Without question, something has a reputation for being bad. Falling into the living God's hands, however, is much worse. I have no idea what it is like to fall into the hands of a living God.

CHAPTER 06
THE TWO INEVITABLE INSTITUTIONS

Is it conceivable for the Church to have legitimate self-government powers? In other words, can America acknowledge a Church as the nation's teacher of religion while still allowing her to manage her own affairs? This right to self-government, which embodies the idea that society, as a whole, can manage its members individually, is divinely granted to the Church. The Church has always maintained this authority, whether it be legislative, disciplinary, or judicial, and no one has ever questioned it. It is supported by the solemn words of Jesus Christ who granted His Church authority and power to preach the gospel, teach, and baptize.

"Jesus approached and, [a]breaking the silence, said to them, All authority (all power of rule) in heaven and on earth has been given to Me." (Matthew 28:18).

The Bible covers four main topics: God, Man, the World as It Is Now, and the World to Come. All other issues are secondary and subordinate to them, and God is supreme. He is not just the God of the Jews but also of the Gentiles. He is the Creator of the World and the Judge of All Nations.

"And He made from one [common origin, one source, one blood] all nations of men to settle on the face of the earth having definitely determined [their] allotted periods of time and the fixed boundaries of their habitation (their settlements, lands, and abodes)" (Acts 17:26).

God has gathered His peculiar people into His church. But those outside are still subject to His moral law and sovereign judgment. Every Christian must understand that they are subject to two divine powers, each in its own domain: the authority of the Church in spiritual issues and the authority of America or other nations in social and political life. And if a Christian is to be a smart person in addition to being a devoted citizen and patriot, they must fully — or at least, adequately — familiarize themselves with the revelation God has made of themselves as recorded in the written word and in the Eternal Word, as well as the commentary on that revelation found in the annals of human history.

Every genuine Christian is an ardent supporter of their country and the government to which they belong. They must carry out their civic responsibilities in their capacity as a Christian; and as a citizen and a patriot, they must exhibit the values of Jesus Christ.

THE WAR OF JURIDICTION

If America or any other State were to pass a law requiring anything to be done that is against the law of God, it would be the Church's duty to discipline any of her members who ought to obey the law. People then have to decide which of the two authorities they would follow based on their own private consciences. The Church has no choice but to exclude them from her fold if they decide to submit to the State. These incidents are seldom ever likely to happen. But the majority of state laws that contradict God's law are those that govern marriage. Practically, they are simply accommodating.

With a few exceptions, the State gives each person the freedom to choose whether or not to get married and, if they do, to marry whoever they want. However, she does not compel someone to marry, much less to marry a specific individual.

When a person enters into a marriage that is against the law of God and not the law of the country, they have committed an offense which is subject to church disciplinary measures.

However, if that person does not enter into such a marriage, he or she neither offends the Church nor the United States of America because the State's law is purely tolerant. It would be more accurate to state that there is no State law on the matter. Therefore, there is no conflict between the Church and the State when a person receives censure from the Church for entering into a marriage that the State does not prohibit. The other forbids what one allows, and everyone subject to both laws must abide by the more restrictive one. Really, there is no issue unless a situation occurs in which one forbids what the other mandates.

Therefore, the laws that permit the termination of a legally binding union and the marriage of its members to other people before any of them dies are basically just lenient. No one is required to seek a divorce, get one, consent to one, or become married again after a divorce. The State does not mandate any of those, and the Church does not incite conflict by outlawing them.

The American Church used to have peculiar laws. Once upon a time, in America, offenses that were not specifically described in the precepts or by any other means than the broadest allusion to the Divine law were subject to its discipline. The result was that the judges overseeing church discipline were responsible for interpreting the Divine law. They had to follow the law of the country, or, as the public opinion's framers prefer to say, they had to obey the law of the land.

When the law of the land did not conflict with the law of God, they were to follow it, but they were not to subordinate the law of God to the law of the land. Because the law of the land has less authority than the law of God, it could not be used to evaluate whether the law of the land conflicts with the law of God. God's law, which is the greater law, had to be the rule, and conscience had to be the judge to enforce it. Everyone who was asked to respond to the question about marriage had to make their own decisions as they had to make their own decisions about every other question.

The individual must make a conscience-based decision. Unless the Church has provided them with a regulation, the officer of the Church who is called to counsel, instruct, or judge the conduct of the private Christian must make his or her decision per his or her own conscience. The Church had to be guided by what can be referred to as her aggregate, or public conscience, in her capacity as a legislator. Each and every person, including Church authority, had to abide by both laws if they did not conflict. Everyone, including Church authority, is required to observe both laws if they do not conflict.

They had to obey God instead of man if one command was something the other forbade. Imagine that a man who had married after receiving a civil divorce and also had a girlfriend besides his wife — which was against God's law — was asked to partake of the Church's communion.

What conduct is expected of the church priest? Given that he had not done anything against the law of the state, the general public (Society) may believe that the twice-married man should be allowed. But the fundamental question is: Has or is he or she still violating God's law? The law of the land, which is, at best, a human interpretation of divine law, was created by human rulers for human ends and has nothing to do with spiritual matters.

America has the right to interpret the law of God for her own ends, but she has no authority to do so for the Church's objectives. She has the authority to decide whether behaviors are detrimental to people's worldly interests but not to the agent's spiritual well-being. Nevertheless, it is well known that many state leaders do not even attempt to interpret God's law. They assert that their only reason for acting is personal expediencies.

Although this is a gross abuse of power, it does not affect America's rightful jurisdiction. To think that her power may be abused and lost would make all governments impossible. The laws of the State are enforceable in State courts, even if they contradict with the law of God.

A judge should resign from their job if their conscience forbids them from carrying out a state law. The second marriage in the alleged case is not polygamy under the law. However, like any other spouse, the husband is legally entitled to control his de facto wife and her assets. According to his ability and situation, the de facto husband is legally required to provide support for the so-called wife. She will be entitled to a wife's portion of his estate when he passes away. The legitimate wife has forfeited her entitlement to financial support and a portion of her husband's assets.

The second marriage's children are legitimately born. All of those outcomes are possible through state regulation. However, the accompanying sin cannot be removed by the State. The Church lacks both the authority and the right to meddle in those civic concerns.

However, she has the right to claim that such a relationship is immoral and harmful to the interests of those involved spiritually. Although a legislative act would be very helpful to specific clerics as a line of defense against public opinion, such an act is not required to proclaim because it would not give more power to a Divine mandate. The true meaning of a legislative act is that it is an explanation of Divine rule, the meaning or application of which may be subject to some debate.

This truth is stated in the following by St. Germain, a veteran author on the Common Law:

"The law of man (which sometimes is called the law positive) is derived by reason as a thing which is necessary and probably following of the law of reason and of the law of God. And that is probable, in that it appears to be true to many, especially to wise men. And therefore, in every law positive well made, there is somewhat of the law of reason, and somewhat of the law of God."

All those who are legally under the control of the people who make laws are bound by them to the extent of their jurisdiction, but no farther. America does not have authority over spiritual concerns, unless it becomes necessary to do so in order to defend herself, her citizens, or her subjects from harm that might be attempted to take on a spiritual shape. Even then, it does not include determining what constitutes sin and what does not. Her interpretation of God's law for this reason lacks validity. The Church is responsible for explaining the law of God for spiritual ends. However, giving a plain Divine law a legislative interpretation is unnecessary. Therefore, the church may yield to interpreting such a Divine rule by her judicial and executive officials. When the State's interpretation conflicts with the genuine meaning of the Divine rule, they are not required to follow it.

Both the Church and the State have jurisdiction over matrimonial causes, each in her own sphere and for her own purposes. One may act concerning the temporal welfare of the community under her care; the other concerning the spiritual welfare of mankind. They enforce their decisions in different ways: one punishes that which she considers as bigamy, by forced labor; the other censures that which, in her judgment, is the same offense by suspension from the Holy Communion. The Church has no right to complain of the State for punishing a man who has married again during the life of a former wife. However, the Church may regard the first marriage as against the Divine law, and void because it was contracted with a brother's widow, or for any other reason. So, the State has no right to complain if the Church censures a man who has married a second time during his wife's life although the State has released him from his civil obligations to her.

There seems, however, to be a notion that questions concerning matrimony are peculiarly within the jurisdiction of the State. Like all other questions, they are within her jurisdiction so far as the temporal welfare of the people and the administration of the temporal laws are concerned; but like all other questions, they are within the jurisdiction of the Church, so far as they bear upon the spiritual welfare of mankind. We suppose the contrary is to fall into the old error which grew out of the old union between Church and State that some questions are, in themselves, of spiritual, and others of temporal jurisdiction; whereas, in truth, all questions of right and wrong belong to both; though each is to treat all questions for her own purposes and in her own manner.

In former times, many attempts were made to settle the questions between the Church and the State by allotting certain causes and questions to one and others to the other. During those attempts, matrimonial causes were assigned to the ecclesiastical courts to be decided according to church law. In many parts of the world, they remained in that position until very lately. They are now held to be of civil jurisdiction in many other countries. They really belong to both, to each within her own sphere, and for her own proper purposes, according to her nature, and the object for which she was instituted.

> *"God's law, which is the greater law, had to be the rule, and conscience had to be the judge to enforce it."*

GOD'S LAW PERMIATES ALL LAWS

Church and State are both under the divine appointment in a certain sense. And the Family fits this description. But in every situation, it is distinct that it is true. A Divine law that has been explicitly revealed governs how the Family is to be structured. The fundamental rules of society have been revealed to the Church. However, many matters are still left to be governed by the Church itself, "according to the diversity of places, periods, and men's ways so that nothing be ordained against God's Word." There has not been much revealed in the bible about the State other than the fact that her existence and recognition are in accordance with the

Divine Will. All other decisions have been left to human law and Divine Providence. There seems to be only one rule:

"Let every person be loyally subject to the governing (civil) authorities. For there is no authority except God [by His permission, His sanction], and those that exist do so by God's appointment." (Romans 13:1).

Both the Church and the State have their rightful domains, and each has authority within those domains. However, because their authority is derived and hence, subordinate, both have limited power. The law of God may be interpreted, applied, and enforced by each within their respective areas. The law is the source of all human authority, thus, neither party should establish any rules that are in conflict with it.

The Church Is Supreme

The Church has jurisdiction over everyone by divine appointment, and everyone is compelled to join the one Church by joining one of her federated societies. However, because she has no other ways of maintaining her authority beyond exclusion from her privileges, which is useless against people who do not want them, she essentially has no members who didn't voluntarily join her. The federated societies that make up the one Church are actually branches that have developed from a single root and are not historically federated, although being so in practice. Although they are, at least, conceptually, spiritually one, they are actually only very loosely connected externally.

Smaller societies are made up of the components that make up the larger society. Those are linked through federations, which are a lot more intimately knit than the vast society. The smaller federations usually have a defined territory within which they have power over all Church members and function as missionary societies to convert anyone who is not a member.

Usually, these borders coincide with those of certain states. There are several differences between the smaller federations, often known as individual churches, and the local states that contain them. They differ in how they are set up, what they are used for, and what things they occupy.

The idea that the Church and the State are two outward manifestations of one society has its roots in the identity of territory and, as a result of the people who should be under the jurisdiction of certain churches with those who are subjects of particular states. The doctrine of the union, or better yet, the oneness of Church and State, is based on this idea. Because all of the members of the two organizations are the same people; it has been claimed that they are essentially two representations of one civilization.

This may be true if it were considered that both organizations were the result of the society itself, but if one of them is a Divine institution, it is not a representation of the society. It is a tool God has appointed for governing and educating society's citizens.

CHAPTER 07

THE PRIVATE CONSCIENCE AND JUDGEMENT

This is the underlying premise of private conscience which is sometimes confused with private judgment and has both a right and duty. Conscience is the understanding that one applies to moral issues, and one is quickly at ease when one's understanding is persuaded that everything is right. Conscience lives within every human being much as judges often sit in chambers while hearing cases in front of cameras in courtrooms. In order to make an accurate judgment of the situation, the godly person's spirit is always prepared to arrange the court of conscience and conduct a solemn trial of their heart and life.

Godly people are helped by conscience to avoid substituting the wicked for the innocent. Conviction is, therefore, brought about by conscience, which also aids in judgment. The two, however, are as different from one another. Any issue can be decided by judgment, including those involving right and wrong as well as purely practical concerns. A fairly typical instance might be used to highlight the difference. One person in authority decides what constitutes a law's correct application. Another person who reports to the former makes an appeal to his (the latter) own private judgment and declares: "You are wrong in your interpretation; I will dismiss it and follow my own." This is unjustified private judgment. However, if a person turns to their conscience and determines that they cannot abide by the law perceived by their superior, they must disobey. While it's debatable whether conscience is an independent faculty or just a function of reason, everyone can agree that judgment is just a reasoned function. Regardless of whether they belong to the same faculty or not, it is obvious that they function in different fields. Conscience can only take action in relation to morality-related concerns, whereas judgment has the power to decide any issue.

"Let every person be loyally subject to the governing (civil) authorities. For there is no authority except God [by His permission, His sanction], and those that exist do so by God's appointment" (Romans 13:1).

A person may surrender their moral judgment to power but not their conscience. They may not act in accordance with man's authority in a way that they are sure is inappropriate in God's eyes. However, if what they are obligated to do by human authority is not against God's law, then their conscience just serves to remind them that they must submit to the authorities that God has placed in charge of them. A person should submit their own judgment to such authority unless it violates God's law.

People should also keep in mind what they all-too-often forget: that their private consciences are totally private and that one man's conscience is neither a guide for another man nor a source of authority for someone who has never been subjected to it by divine power. The office of private conscience determines if human law is in conflict with divine law. Its office determines its boundaries; as in other situations, a right cannot go beyond the foundational ideas upon which it is based.

Private conscience has the responsibility of determining whether a lesser law is so incompatible with a greater one that it is impossible to obey one without violating the other - only the person whose conscience will benefit from this action. People must obey the stricter law when both cannot be followed because it mandates something that the other bans. The higher law must be followed when a private person's conscience tells them that this is the case; nonetheless, everyone else is entitled to the same freedom of inquiry and self-determination.

No private individual has the right to dictate to another. A private person also has no right to enquire beyond the legitimacy, so to speak, of the subordinate law. The Word speaks about individual conscience that "…We must obey God rather than men" (Acts 5:29). Private conscience, therefore, has no rights in situations where it is possible to obey both. A person does not serve the private will. Men often overlook this and confuse it with their own private preferences, whim, and judgment.

To determine whether a private person, or possibly a public officer, is required to obey the law as interpreted by human authority, or, as it is more commonly phrased, to obey a human law or follow a human decision, private judgment is typically applied. It typically comes into play when someone is hesitant to follow the letter of the law or accept how the law has been interpreted.

Her voice is heard when she chooses to act of her own free will, as she typically does in these situations. She has gained a lot of friends thanks to the liberality of her decisions, despite her false claim to use private judgment.

Almost everyone supports using one's own discretion. The decisions of the individual conscience should be taken fairly with due consideration and within the boundaries of its legitimate domain. Above all, they ought to be created with a strong feeling of obligation to God and His Law. In these circumstances, the final authority on human conduct is each man's conscience.

Generally, questions about the conscience's authority can be answered by keeping in mind that its role in public law is to stop lesser authorities from overturning those of their superiors. It must resolve all issues involving authority. People are able to expand and retain this function of the conscience even when it conflicts with private judgment and renders judgments on matters of taste and expediency. This is because they may ingeniously escape obeying any authority while protected by it.

Unfortunately, it has another office that is currently very crucial. It might merely be a variation of the other - to make a decision between organizations that pose as the Church but do not follow God's commands.

The Church, having no right or power to apply external force, cannot prevent the formation of other organizations which assume her name and claim her authority. Private conscience must make a decision between the disputing claims based on the case's need. Every man is required by the law of God to join the true Church. Each of the two groups asserts to be that Church. The person who wants to join either must then choose for themselves which is the right choice; that is, which of them is abiding by Divine rule and which is not.

The private conscience also serves in another capacity, but few people take advantage of it. To put it another way, a kind conscience is a great asset; yet, many people are unaware of its worth. It involves interpreting and using the Divine rule to guide one's behavior in situations where no equivalent human law exists. When conscience acts as a restraint in this situation, people respond to it much less favorably than when it acts as a liberator from restraint by using the mask of private judgment.

This function heavily relies on conscience because no human law actually interprets or applies the fullness of the Divine law — nor does it even attempt to do so. The Divine law is only enforced to the extent that the State deems it essential for the temporal wellbeing of her citizens or subjects. She duplicates those and imposes human penalties. Many churches claim to uphold the entirety of the Divine law. But aside from a very small amount, she has not interpreted it in a legislative format.

Many churches typically leave the legal interpretation to their judicial authorities that do so as cases warrant. They even give them a lot of leeway when it comes to applying human penalties to enforce the law. Some people have been misled by this believing the Church has adopted the State's interpretation. But no church, real or imagined, has ever done this. The State's interpretations are developed for her own ends which differ greatly from those the Church must uphold. Because of this, they are completely insufficient for the Church's needs. In addition, many State laws lack any connection to the law of God and are based only on concepts of pragmatism. Once more, State laws are simply intended to protect men in temporal affairs. Just because something is sinful does not faze them. All of those factors make it impossible for any good church to adopt the tenet that it is constrained by how the State interprets the divine law.

In interpreting and applying that element of the Divine rule that has not been the subject of a public interpretation to men's private action, a very wide area is left for individual conscience. This aspect of the Divine law is commonly referred to as morals or morality. Its name derives from the Latin word "mores," which means "customs" or "usages", because societal norms heavily influence men's ideas regarding it. The Latin word mores is equivalent to the two words we have in English: morals and manners. We use the first to describe practices that immediately impact society as a whole and are generally accepted to require some form of divine law, whether revealed or natural. The second is used to describe usages that solely impact certain circles' comfort and are correctly believed to be regulated by the opinions of such circles.

The Divine rule should govern morals and manners, and it is the responsibility of the private conscience to apply and uphold this law. Society has created public opinion in order to free it from that task.

Formally, private conscience rules in the area of manners and effectively in the area of public opinion. It is vitally important to note that morality does not equal righteousness; morality may only be cleansing the outside of the cup and platter while the heart may be filled with wickedness. Righteousness excludes immorality, but morality does not equal righteousness. Righteousness deals with men's intentions, goals, objectives, objects, and motives. Righteousness requires that the heart be fixed on God and that it should beat with love toward Him. Where morality only scratches the surface of the immense deep; righteousness enters the very caverns of the great depth. It is possible for a moral person to be fully moral without being righteous.

Morality is a lovely, a beautiful corpse that has been properly dressed, bathed, and even embalmed with spices. However, righteousness is a living person who is just as beautiful and fair as the other but alive also. While righteousness waits and pants with high aspirations, ready to mount and live in immortality beyond the stars, morality lies there, earthly, soon-to-be food for corruption and worms. These two are diametrically opposed in nature; one is of this earth, and the other is of the world beyond the heavens.

> "... There is still a temple on Earth, but it is not one
> built by human hands.— a temple reared,
> not by human masons, hewers of stone,
> carpenters, and other artificers,
> but built by God Himself. This temple
> is the Church of God."

The Dual Role Of The Conscience

The Church and the United States of America are two institutions with separate foundations but equal authority granted by God. America has jurisdiction over everyone found inside her borders, including Church members; the Church has jurisdiction over her own members.

When circumstances place an action within their respective realms, each has authority over that action. Because of this, the two societies exist for opposite reasons — one for the sake of eternity and the other for the sake of humanity's present well-being. Any conceivable activity may fall under the purview of either. Because no voluntary action can be taken, that won't have an impact on the agent's spiritual well-being or another person's temporal well-being.

Many actions are under both the Church's and America's purview at the same time. Therefore, there must be a risk of collisions between the two societies. However, there is no risk of contact between the two places. The Church has no authority over anything or anyone who isn't a member of her. However, the Church has a separate authority that may be used without regard for the government's choices.

"[Now having received the Holy Spirit, and being [b] led and directed by Him] if you forgive the sins of anyone, they are forgiven; if you retain the sins of anyone, they are retained" (20:23).

"Obey your spiritual leaders and submit to them [continually recognizing their authority over you], for they are constantly keeping watch over your souls and guarding your spiritual welfare, as men who will have to render an account [of their trust]. [Do your part to] let them do this with gladness and not with sighing and groaning, for that would not be profitable to you [either]" (Hebrews 13:17).

She may pass laws that are in line with those of America's, in which case, her authority will support that of the State; alternatively, she may pass laws that are in conflict with those of the State, in which case, the two authorities will be at odds.

History teaches us that the Roman emperors were hostile toward the early church. They exerted all of their power against her, but they were unable to overthrow the Christian Church. The worst actions taken by the Roman emperors were all in vain. King Herod did same to the Church. He murdered James and tried to murder Peter.

"About that time, Herod the king stretched forth his hands to afflict and oppress and torment some who belonged to the church (assembly). And he killed James the brother of John with a sword; And when he saw that it was pleasing to the Jews, he proceeded further and arrested Peter also. This was during the days of Unleavened Bread [the Passover week]" (Acts 12:1-3).

The Jews afflicted the Church and drove her from city to city. Then Saul of Tarsus, who eventually became Paul, afflicted the church by inhaling threats and murder against her.

"Meanwhile Saul, [a]still drawing his breath hard from threatening and murderous desire against the disciples of the Lord, went to the high priest" (Acts 9:1).

Then the widespread persecution of Pagans began. Christians were executed with a variety of methods, including tearing them to pieces, allowing them to languish in jail, torturing them on a rack, and putting them to death. Because the two societies are independent of each other and from the God who appointed them both and from whom both societies get their authority, this conflict is possible. Because fallible men administer both, it is feasible that the two authorities will reach contrary conclusions. Either one or both could interpret the Divine law incorrectly. God has, however, also limited each of them to their rightful domain. Neither party has the authority to interfere with the other's decisions or prevent each other from enforcing their respective decisions.

Honorable individuals run either one or both, and neither may adhere to the divine law. Therefore, America or any other country is not obligated to accept the Church's law as a justification for breaking her (the State) laws. Similarly, the Church is not required to accept State law as justification for breaking her (the Church) own laws. In addition, neither party should try to adapt their respective laws to those of the other. Their respective laws serve distinct functions and are upheld by various punishments. Everyone who is under the authority of both must submit to both. Each person must independently choose which rule they will follow in a conflict, per the dictates of their conscience. Which of the two is consistent with the law of God is a decision left up to the conscience.

If one's conscience cannot provide an answer, then everyone must decide between temporal benefits and church privileges, as well as between church censure and temporal punishment. The Church has been given the power to advance the spiritual well-being of humanity since it is a formally structured community. In the divine plan, she is both Catholic and universal. Her mission is to unite all peoples under her sphere of influence.

To accomplish this, she must be so pure that men can see her and be drawn to her like a city on a hill that cannot be hidden.

"You are the light of the world. A city set on a hill cannot be hidden" (Matthew 5:14).

Jesus Christ prayed for a unique group of people during His time on earth. He passionately stated that He did not make an intercession for everyone. He said:

"You are the light of the world. A city set on a hill cannot be hidden." (John 17:9).

When we read this lovely prayer in its entirety, we can only think of one question: Who are the people referred to as "them" or "they"? Who are those special people Jesus prays for, acknowledged by His love, and whose names are inscribed on the stones of His precious breastplate? Who are those people whose characteristics and situations are mentioned by the High Priest before the throne of heaven? The answer to that question is supplied throughout the bible. The people for whom Jesus Christ prays are not of this world. They are a people who exist slightly apart from the rest of the world:

"They are not of the world [worldly, belonging to the world], just as I am not of the world" (John 17:16) *"They are a city set on a hill."*

CHAPTER 08

GENDER RELATIONS

Although the legislation governing marriage and the relationship between the sexes are two distinct topics, they are so closely related that one cannot be discussed without referencing the other. Therefore, it is appropriate to mention the other topic while looking into the Christian view of marriage. As it is with most other moral issues, there is some scriptural truth and several false theories regarding the relationship between the sexes (Man and Woman).

The most critical component of social structures in the history of the world is the gender relationship between the sexes. Society is typically in a sound state when sound ideas on the topic are dominant. Conversely, where sexist stereotypes are prevalent, societal structures are typically unfavorable.

Any thoughtful human being in every civilized nation can see the state of the turmoil of sexes that currently permeates our world. In one way or another, there is a feeling of confusion, and it is becoming clear that in some situations, what has long stewed as a complaint cannot be prevented from erupting into aggressive antagonism.

The conflict between the sexes is family warfare, and just as family turmoil causes the worst conflicts, the conflict between the sexes has the potential to cause animosity that might linger for years and do enormous harm to our world. Most of the world's population are overwhelmed since sex-based warfare seems to be a brand-new experience. However, the Bible's revelation of theology serves as a solace because it is the only accurate theology regarding gender relations.

The Bible does a good job of explaining gender relations in general. Any deviation from the biblical teaching on gender relations is considered a false theory. A false theory finds its core because it has strayed from the great, essential, beautiful truth of gender relations. For the purposes of the book's content, I shall focus on five of the many false theories that abound on Gender relations. Most false theories have the advantage of being based on a theory about the origin of women from the Bible.

*"The conflict between the sexes is family warfare,
and just as family turmoil causes the worst conflicts,
the conflict between the sexes has the potential to cause
animosity that might linger for years and
do enormous harm to our world."*

FALSE THEORIES OF MARRIAGE

One of the theories holds that God created women to solve sin and prevent sexual immorality so that Adam and all males may get married and maintain their purity. The holders of this view dwell on God's proclamation after He had created the woman to mean she was only created for procreation (Genesis 3:16).

Another almost similar theory holds that aside from the brief period of time needed for both sexes to contribute to the survival of the human race, women and men are to live and develop separately from each other. According to this perspective, the wife is similar to a business partner. It assumes that the roles, obligations, and responsibilities of the sexes should be the same and that they only differ in the ways that the lower animals do.

The obvious implication of those theories is that sexual union should only occur for the sole goal of procreation. Sexual union is not the only end but a necessary one. However, it is unacceptable to regard sexual union as a goal in and of itself. Because it implies that married couples should only engage in sexual activity for procreation.

Another misconception is that women were made to serve as men's objects of sensual pleasure. This notion claims that a woman is a pawn. It is common among half-civilized countries that have advanced in sensuous sophistication. Despite not only being used in the crudest sense, women are also still seen as a source of sensual pleasure. In other words, so that a woman might be more capable and ready to provide pleasure, she is to be complimented, nurtured, and adorned. Rarely acknowledged, it lurks in every level of society, not the least of which is the top. The basis for most sexual immorality is this idea.

The truth - of which it is a misinterpretation - is that woman was meant to be more than just a helpmeet to man; she was not created to be a mere worker in servitude. If women were created to be just gofers, then it stands to reason that they are slaves. These ideas are prevalent in societies with underdeveloped intellects and sympathies. And they are enforced by the superior strength and courage of a man.

There is also a theory that women are superior to men and that they were created to be ornamental, nurturing, and charming. This is fairly contemporary and pervasive. According to this concept, a wife is an idol. Therefore, Men are expected to respect women as being naturally superior to the latter. Although a man cannot sincerely hold it and is seldom ever taken seriously by a woman, it, nonetheless, has some influence on the opinions of the majority of women and many young men. It has the potential to greatly contributing to social evil. It is simply all other false theories in a more civilized form that have been reproduced and developed. As far as it goes, that is factual and only false because it lacks certain information. It is not true that the preservation of life is the ultimate cause of women. Each of the others is founded on the fallacious idea that women were created for a domestic environment.

Although it has been argued that partial truths are complete lies, this is not even close to being true. But the most intriguing idea of them all is a widely held belief that sex doesn't exist; that neither men nor women exist. A sensible person would find it impossible to accept such an ideology as true. To presume that all men are women and all women are males is shocking, unchristian, and detrimental to the concept of marriage, family, church, and state. However, it has made a considerable impact on the attitudes and actions of a certain group of people who don't try to organize their thoughts into doctrines and are willing to discuss the Bible without using it as their personal guide.

The idle conversation among the members of this class shapes their opinions more than any firmly held beliefs from the Bible. Many misguided doctrines and inhumane practices enter society as a result of those heretical theories that have been proliferating. Those false conceptions about women have given rise to unethical marriage practices. The historical mistakes gave rise to polygamy, wrongful marriages between the sexes, forced marriage of women, and divorce at the spouse's discretion. Modernity has led to an increasing number of divorces, separations by consent that truly result in divorce, revolt against marriage, and marital problems on a global scale.

SHE IS HELPMEET, NOT HELPMATE

The biblical concept of marriage is originally mentioned in the first few chapters of Genesis and is further elaborated in subsequent books of the Bible which it permeates. The answer is that a woman was made to be a wife and a mother and that her role as a wife is to support, counsel, and help her husband who is in charge of her.

A godly woman considers it a great honor that a godly and honorable man would choose her out of all the other women in the world to be his wife. When a man asks a woman to be his wife, he elevates her to a queenly status. The man prostrates himself at the woman's feet and elevates her to the throne of his life. He gives the woman a lot of power and confides in her the guardianship of holy destinies. Her marital life may hold the key to determining if a woman wears her crown virtuously and blesses and beautifies her monarchy.

Because of their differences, the man and the woman fill the gaps left by the other. Each completes and complements the other. A virtuous woman married to a nobleman is Heaven's final and finest gift to humanity and, thus, to the world. The woman is the man's angel, a channel for numerous blessings, and a jewel for countless virtues.

The correct role of a wife has not been left up to any theory of inference.

The role of a wife is explicitly stated as being that of her husband's companion and helpmeet in carrying out his responsibilities. The woman is a helpmeet, not a master. Because of the differences between her animal, intellectual, emotional, and moral natures and those of the male, she is more suited for those roles.

Her smiles are the light of his day, and her voice is the loveliest melody to him. Her kiss protects a man's integrity; her hands provide security; and her touch is a guaranteed medicine for his life. A woman's industry and economy are the safest guardians of her husband's fortune. She is also the mother of his children; therefore, it makes sense that her lips serve as his trusted advisor. A woman's prayers are the most effective advocates for Heaven's blessing on her husband's head, and her husband rests on the sweetest pillow of his worries in her bosom. Because her husband enjoys her company more, she is a more valuable companion.

Like all other communities, a family needs a head, which implies that all other members must submit to the man or the woman. By divine appointment, the man is the head of the family, and the woman is the deputy of the family. The woman's moral makeup very well suits her for the submissive role that has been given to her.

"So God created man in his own image, male and female, created He them. And God blessed them, and said unto them, be fruitful and multiply, and replenish the earth and subdue it." (Genesis 1:27-28).

Interestingly, this earliest mention of woman has a hint that she fulfills or completes the image of man, without which it is incomplete "…in the image of God created He him", and then immediately, "male and female created He them."

God gave a reason for creating a woman, "And the Lord God said, it is not meet for man to be alone: I will make a helpmeet for him." In relation to God's explanation, it is important to note that the word "meet" which means "fit" or "proper" has left the common language. Because of this, the phrase has been misunderstood, which has given rise to the widespread usage of the term "helpmate" for a wife. It is not improbable that some incorrect teaching could be concealed within this common phrase and the confusion surrounding it.

God's phrase's genuine intent does not imply equality; rather, it states that He would provide Adam with an assistant that should suit him. He reveals His motivations in each and every mention of the creation of women in the Bible. The relationship between the sexes can be deduced from them.

God created women for various reasons which can be summed up in three key areas: to serve and support man while ensuring the human race's procreation. A woman will logically act as a man's friend if she were acting as her helper. Her nature must be the counterpart to his, filling in the gaps where he is lacking in order that these functions are performed. It is found to be a case of a marriage that is divinely appointed. (Genesis 1:27, 28/2:18).

"A woman's prayers are the most effective advocates for Heaven's blessing on her husband's head, and her husband rests on the sweetest pillow of his worries in her bosom."

A Contemporary Helpmeet (Adam And Eve)

In order that I may make this matter very plain and maybe the more likely to enlist your attention and to secure the friendship of your memories in future years, I intend to use President Joseph R. Biden, the president of the United States of America, as the Father of the world's family household, and vice president Kamala Harris as the mother of the home.

President Joseph R. Biden and Vice President Kamala Harris are to form a society with children, when born, which would require a head. The headship belongs to President Joe Biden, vice president Kamala Harris is the deputy, and the American Citizens are the children. But as Kamala Harris was created as President Biden's companion, there cannot be a very wide interval between them. Yet, Kamala Harris' position as a help implies subordination.

The third relation inferred from those two is that Kamala Harris is the counselor or adviser to President Biden. She is not designed to govern him; one who helps does not direct the work. It is not her office to overrule President Joseph R. Biden's judgment by authority, by violence, or by persuasion. But Kamala Harris is to present for President Biden consideration that side of every question which the intellectual and moral constitution of her sex enables her to see more clearly than he can. Vice President Kamala Harris is designed to be President Biden's counselor, but in that, as in every other relation, to be subordinate to him.

WOMEN'S ROLES ARE DISTINCT FROM MEN'S

Even in Eden, men were in the authority of women. Subordination is inequality used to maintain order. According to the established hierarchy of things, a subordinate position is one that is beneath another. The inferior position of a woman means that she has a different makeup from that of men, one that is better suited to a lower sphere of influence rather than any lack or shortcoming in her physical, intellectual, or moral constitution.

When we delve so deeply into the Creator's plan, it is clear that there is a difference between men and women. All evidence points to basic differences between the natures of men and women. They are distinct in thought and character. The spiritual distinctions are only a type and reflection of the physical ones.

If they are not suppressed by intellectual theories and hypotheses, all human instincts indicate that some characteristics make a man's character the most admirable and certain characteristics make a woman's character the most lovable and alluring.

It is impossible to switch between these unique trails. Under no circumstances can a man change into a woman or a woman into a man. What is best in one may be very opposite in another. The two were designed from birth and by nature for entirely different roles in life. Each person has unique responsibilities and a distinct area of expertise.

Although equal, men and women are not the same. Despite being unlike each other, they are nonetheless equal. Each possesses characteristics that the other does not. Each is tailored to the specific duties that the other cannot, or at the very least, cannot perform as well. They work together in unison. Both are essential for completing the genuine picture of mankind. The Bible seems to teach this clearly. Along with the fact that he was produced in the likeness and image of God, the man was created as both a male and female. These two important realities are juxtaposed in a way that gives the impression that they are one and the same. Because man was created as both a male and female, there can be no dispute that they are inseparable or made in God's likeness. The vast collection of people—in this world and the next—who live according to divine order and are the willing receptacles and conduits of the divine influence is the fullest and purest image of the Lord, not a single person, however far along the path of regenerate life.

Man is one half of this vast human race, and woman is the other. It goes without saying that the image would be severely damaged, if not completely obliterated, if those two portions were to be removed from each other.

Both the feminine and the masculine features are required to complete the likeness. In the same way, a man and a woman who are happily married together makeup God's likeness and image more perfectly than either of them could do on their own. The spiritual perspective of God is the most accurate. Of all the living creatures, only man most closely resembles his Heavenly Father.

Therefore, a man's truest likeness can be seen in his united soul with a woman. Jesus Christ is the epitome of wisdom and love. His likeness is a vessel for God's love, power, and wisdom "…Christ [is] the Power of God and the Wisdom of God" (1 Corinthians 1:24).

We need to go very far to see that, at least, on the level of life visible to us, man is primarily a repository for wisdom, and woman is mostly a repository for love. Understanding tends to take the lead in the distinctively masculine features, whereas will or attachment tends to do so in the distinctively feminine features. Her feelings and emotions more often guide women, while his judgment and reason more often guide men.

However, they are correspondingly dominated by the two classes of faculties that fall under those headings. And when men and women work together in a positive and ordered manner, they each give the other exactly what is needed. Each fills in the gaps left by the other. They complete a man's form to a higher standard.

Let us put it this way: The heart is Eve in the little marriage garden. She is the one who willfully chooses the fruit, and while understanding comes after affections, just as Adam did after Eve, the first source of power for good or evil is in the affections. However, it is not true that only males possess intelligence and only females possess affection. The issue's core is that the Lord God divided the creature He created into two parts—male and female—that are fundamentally different from each other but remarkably well-suited to each other. The story of Eden's garden and Adam and Eve's early lifestyle there captures the noble and exalted character of the men who made up the first family, church, and community.

In symbolic terms, the serpent's temptation and Adam and Eve's disobedience in eating the forbidden fruit showed how the church started to lose her original purity and innocence. In other words, if subordination didn't already exist in Eden, it might have been instituted just after the Fall.

"To the woman He said, I will greatly multiply your grief and your suffering in pregnancy and the pangs of childbearing; with spasms of distress you will bring forth children. Yet your desire and craving will be for your husband, and he will rule over you." (Genesis 3:16).

This law is completely acknowledged in the New Testament which has numerous passages related to it. Those scriptures largely discuss the duties of a wife to her husband, but the final cause of this relationship between the sexes and that of husband and wife can be stated to be the close connection between the two. (Genesis 2:16).

Still, plenty of scriptures advocate for the subordination of all feminine sexes, not only the wife to the husband. The general exclusion of women from positions of political authority is based on this ideology:

"I would have you know that the head of every man is Christ, and the head of the woman is the man, and the head of Christ is God. Having his head covered, every man praying or prophesying dishonors his head. But every woman that prays or prophesies with her head uncovered dishonors her head; for that is even all one as if she were shaven. For if the woman be not covered, let her also be shorn; but if it is a shame for a woman to be shorn or shaven, let her be covered. For a man indeed ought not to cover his head, forasmuch as he is the image and glory of God; but the woman is the glory of the man. For the man is not of the woman, but the woman of the man. Neither was the man created for the woman, but the woman for the man." (1 Corinthians 11:3-8 NKJV).

"Now the Lord God said. It is not good (sufficient, satisfactory) that the man should be alone; I will make him a helper (suitable, adapted, complementary) for him. (Genesis 2:18).

Although the relationship between a husband and wife is not mentioned in this passage, the teaching of the inequality of the sexes is clearly taught:

"For the man is not of the woman; but the woman of the man. Neither was the man created for the woman, but the woman for the man." (1 Corinthians 11:8-9).

The same apostle reiterates his call for gender inequality in a subsequent letter.

"But if there is anything they want to learn, they should ask their own husbands at home, for it is disgraceful for a woman to talk in church [for her to usurp and exercise authority over men in the church]." (1 Corinthians 14:35).

It is very important to note that CHRISTIANITY is the special friend of women. It has exalted her almost infinitely above the position to which the fall might have assigned her. This elevation began with God's peculiar wisdom ordaining that Jesus Christ should be the woman's son, not the man's. God in His wisdom devised that the woman, and the woman alone, should be the author of the body of the Godman who would redeem mankind, just as the woman, by her daring spirit, stepped first into transgression — lest she be scorned and trampled on.

Despite the fact that she was the one who initially tasted the cursed fruit and enticed her husband (maybe Adam, out of love for her), tasted that fruit).Lest the woman be degraded, lest she not stand on equal footing with him, God decreed that His Son be born "of a woman, and the first promise was that the seed of the woman, not the seed of the man, would crush the serpent's head as expressed in the verse below:

"And I will put enmity between you and the woman, and between your offspring and her Offspring; He will bruise and tread your head underfoot, and you will lie in wait and bruise His heel."(Genesis 3:15)

And during His time on earth, Jesus Christ did not discourage women from becoming disciples; rather, He warmly welcomed them wherever He preached. He gave women the same access to His wisdom, teachings and valuable promises of eternal life as He did to the most admired of men in all their fullness. The status of women rises as Christianity influences increasingly shape society and as the gospel spirit permeates the population.

In modern society, women are no longer regarded as slaves who must carry all the burdens, as they were in prehistoric times, nor are they merely servants or ministers of sensual pleasure, as they still are in many cultures. The harem's doors have been unbarred, and Christianity has pulled the covering from the woman's face. Now a woman can dine at the same table as the men in the family. She can keep her guests entertained and enjoy their company.

She attends the same school as her brothers, takes the same classes, and reads the same textbooks. By adopting and upholding biblical truth, women's roles have been considerably elevated in Christian countries, and they now hold their proper positions. A woman can participate in the sanctuary's service, song, and worship with her friends, engage in conversation in social gatherings, and hear eminent speakers debate literature, art, science, or statesmanship while she also listens to them.

Women who feel moved by the cries of the suffering human race and are passionate about the significant efforts being made to raise the race are allowed to do so. Society acknowledged the influence and authority of women and believed they had both obligations and rights. Detestable laws have gradually been repealed; her property rights have been substantially upheld. Women now have more opportunities for usefulness, and their voices on stage and in the press are welcomed. In this way, the story is explicated.

The essential inference it draws regarding the matter at hand is that humans have always existed as men and women, that this was the precise order of their creation, and that it is required for their welfare and enjoyment.

"He replied, Have you never read that He Who made them from the beginning made them male and female, And said, For this reason a man shall leave his father and mother and shall be united firmly (joined inseparably) to his wife, and the two shall become one flesh?" (Matthew 19:4,5).

Therefore, it follows that a woman must recognize and accept the role that has been allocated to her in God's word in order to put herself in her rightful place and in the best relationships for her to reach her highest elevation, greatest usefulness, and genuine destiny.

They Are A King And A Queen

According to the Bible's teaching on the relationship between the sexes, a woman is a man's equal companion, submissive helper, and advisor. The Hebrew word for help is quite similar to the word used in Genesis to describe the relationship between a woman and a man.

God created Eve to be Adam's helpmeet, and the Holy Spirit has been to every Christian as suitable a help as the helpmeet He created for man. The Holy Spirit is like and even more than a close friend who has been our best help on earth. She is a friend that offers help that is specifically catered for his requirements in the nicest and most joyful manner conceivable. We find in the Holy Spirit the kind of help He requires—help that is compassionately, thoughtfully, and divinely adapted to meet our needs. He responds to our needs and wants and is a constant source of support, providing strength for our frailty, insight for our foolishness, and consolation for our sadness.

God determined to create a bride and a beloved companion for Adam since His great purpose was for him to find a helpmeet. And the woman's nature is made to be his complement, or completion, to fit her for all of those roles. The fundamental nature of the sexes preordains these relationships and exists in an embryonic stage independent of marriage. (1 Corinthians 6: 3-8, 1 Timothy 2:11, 12).

When the apostle Paul preaches about the subjection of women, he takes care to avoid leaving too many unintended interpretations; he adds: "Neither is the man without the woman, neither the woman without the man in the Lord".

"For as the woman is of the man, even so, is the man also by the woman; but all things of God." (1 Corinthians 11:12).

Over again, throughout the Bible, the idea that a woman completements or completes the nature of man is being acknowledged. Her subordination suggests inequality, but it's a limited kind of inequality that does not make her insignificant and is not very severe. These things have been set in place by God in accordance with the hallowed state of matrimony, according to His infinite wisdom. The acceptance of those principles is crucial for the practical holiness of that state. If a man crowns a woman a queen by marrying her, then he is naturally a king. And the word of a king in his kingdom has to be, in a sense, absolute. Not necessary to do everything according to their own will, and none can check them. But the subjects of a godly king who rules his kingdom in fear of God must willingly and gladly submit to him.

The Soul Of Man Plus Woman's Equals The Likeness Of God

Although men and women are equal, they are not alike. Even though they differ, they are, nonetheless, equal. Each has characteristics that the other does not. Each is tailored to the specific duties that the other cannot perform or, at the very least, cannot complete as well. They work together in unison. A man and a woman are needed for the fullest possible representation of humanity. That is a lesson that the Bible makes abundantly clear. It clearly emphasizes that God created both man and woman. Adam is a term that refers to both genders.

"He created them male and female and blessed them and named them [both] Adam [Man] at the time they were created." (Genesis 5:2)

The fact that God made both male and female humans go hand in hand with the truth that He created them in His image and likeness. Those two important principles are presented in a way that makes them appear to be intertwined.

Man and woman are created in the image and likeness of God; thus, male and female are inseparable because God created them for that very purpose, and no one can deny that. No individual, no matter how far along the path of regenerating life they have progressed, embodies God's fullest and truest image. This great human race is made up of two halves, a man and a woman.

Contrary to popular opinion, there are about equal numbers of men and women in the world, although men have a tiny advantage, with 102 men for every 100 women (in 2020). More specifically, out of 1,000 people, 504 (50.4%) are men, and 496 (49.6%) are women (49.6 percent). Males have a larger risk of death than females do, both during childhood and as adults, with 106 boys born for every 100 girls.

Therefore, the proportions of males and females equalize with age. This happens in France at age 25. It goes without saying that if these two pieces were to be separated from one another in any way, the image would be severely damaged, if not completely obliterated. For the likeness to be complete, both masculine and feminine features are needed. In the same way, a man and a woman who are happily married together makeup God's likeness and image more perfectly than either of them could do on their own.

"In the same way, a man and a woman who are happily married together makeup God's likeness and image more perfectly than either of them could do on their own."

God's Word Sustains The Soul Of Man

The closest thing to God's own life is the spiritual life of humans. When God created the beasts of the field, *"He caused the grass to grow for the cattle." (Genesis 1:11)*. He never created a bird without also giving it the seeds or the insects it would eat to survive. Since this is so obviously true, it would be impossible for Him to create spiritual life—which is the closest thing to His own in that it is God's life in man—without making provisions for its continuation, growth, development, and perfection.

In the Garden of Eden, God provided man with His knowledge as the best food. It appears to be God's favorite way of expressing

His image in humans. It originates from God's generous heart and is consistent with the provisions He has established for us, as well as the constant longing for friendship that the great Father has for His children.

After the fall, man, who was made in the image of God and had previously eaten fruits that grew in God's paradise, started to eat things other than the knowledge of God (Hosea 12:1). However, God's grace will not permit His people to behave thus foolishly.

He gave Jesus Christ, the Revealer of God's knowledge, to the world:

"At that time Jesus began to say, I thank You, Father, Lord of heaven and earth [and I acknowledge openly and joyfully to Your honor], that You have hidden these things from the wise and clever and learned, and revealed them to babies [to the childish, untaught, and unskilled] (Matthew 11:25).

The Word is both a source of knowledge about God and food for the soul. We are able to take God's knowledge internally into our souls with the help of the Holy Spirit. Hearing the Word of God is analogous to buying a loaf of bread from the bakery. The act of cutting the bread and putting it on the plate is like meditating on the Word of God. However, this will never satisfy the needs of any soul, just as we must eat the bread into our inner organs in order to digest and assimilate it. So, too, must a person by faith eat the Word and absorb it into their innermost being in order to make what was once outside of them into something that sustains them.

Everything we learn and understand affects our character in some manner much like the flavor of eating an animal's flesh. A persistent observation of anything, whether good or bad, reflects accordingly on us. That is especially true of the spiritual nature that God has given His people during the process of rebirth. We are, therefore, made in the image of the One who created us by consuming the Word which is the knowledge of God.

Man Is Predominantly Intelligent, Woman Predominantly Affectionate

A spiritual image of God is the most accurate representation of Him in humans. When the human soul is properly nourished, it bears the only real and enduring resemblance to God. Thus, the manifestation of God's most perfect resemblance is seen in the combined minds of men and women.

God is Love and wisdom in their purest forms. His likeness is a vessel for His Love and wisdom. God is Love, and those who are not divinely enlightened lack knowledge of God. Those who know God naturally have a pet name for Him much like a loving spouse who gives their lover a nickname. When the Israelites finally understood who God really was, they gave Him the loving name *Ishi*, which means "my husband". A true husband and a wife are complementary to each other and have a mutually committed relationship.

Experience in life, at least, that which is observable, has shown that a woman is primarily a reservoir of Love, and a man is foremost a reservoir of wisdom. Men's distinctively masculine qualities are those in which intelligence takes the starring role. The features that make a woman distinctly feminine are those in which volition or affection takes precedence. The woman is more often guided by her feelings and perceptions while the man is more often guided by his judgment and reason.

This is not meant to imply that all intelligence belongs to men and all affection to women. However, they are correspondingly dominated by the two classes of faculties that fall under those headings. And when men and women work together in a positive and an ordered manner, they each give the other exactly what is needed. They compensate for each other's shortcomings. They complete mankind in a complete way. They are quite like Adam and Eve in the Garden. Adam is the understanding in a marriage, while Eve is the affection. And they both complement each other nicely in a marital relationship. In these apparently complex relationships, each modifies the others, and the others modify one another.

Equality in one capacity affects the subordination in another, and the subordination, in turn, modifies and softens the equality. Since the two concepts are intertwined, neither is absolute nor unaffected by the other. Such is the subordination of women, and such is the equality of the genders.

"A spiritual image of God is the most accurate of Him in humans."

A MAN AND A WOMAN COMPLEMENT EACH OTHER

A thin, razor-thin line must exist between lying, expressing a woman's equality with a man in an unguarded way, and exaggerating a woman's submissiveness. Some people use a scale that allows for a mile to equal an inch when discussing a woman's submission to a man. They are, without comparison, abhorrent, and they are described as terrible. They are set up in such a way that women's equality has been overlooked, and her subordination has been emphasized.

Therefore, it is essential to put protections around the woman. They are contained in the revealed laws governing the exclusivity and irrevocability of marriage, which have been given by the divine authority. Any mind can often find comfort in protection. One of the many ways that God's law defends women is found in the scripture below:

"In the same way you married men should live considerately with [your wives], with an intelligent recognition [of the marriage relation], honoring the woman as [physically] the weaker, but [realizing that you] are joint heirs of the grace (God's unmerited favor) of life, in order that your prayers may not hindered and cut off. [Otherwise you cannot pray effectively.] (1 Peter 3:7).

We normally come across perplexing opinions and, at other times, we struggle to balance God's law and the freedom of human institutions. It is best to avoid delving too deeply into those deep waters for fear of becoming lost in despair. "The Lord knows" how to protect His own. God has a point of reconciliation regarding all the profound truths He has revealed. Although it appears to be inferred by the revelation's overall tone, a third of great importance is not revealed in full. It is a woman's right to choose her own husband. This should go as far as prohibiting any woman from being forced against her choice to accept a man as her husband.

Divorce, polygamy, forced marriage, and the seclusion of the first two requirements have all played a significant role in the devaluation of women. The practice of kidnapping women and selling them as slaves is also defensible. God Himself consequently established the fact that a man should only have one female companion. A woman is to serve as a man's helper, his representative in the administration of his family, and the object of his undivided affection.

A Woman's Approval Is Essential

Abraham sent Eleazar of Damascus to find a wife for his Son Isaac. Before beginning his task, the obedient servant of Abraham made contact with his master to clarify things with him. The veteran servant then left to complete his hard and challenging task.

After taking all necessary precautions, Eleazer entrusted his case to the wise judgment of both his own and his master's God. His efforts, which were completely in line with his faith and divine predictions, were immediately blessed by success.

God providentially sent Rebecca, the woman who would make the best wife for Isaac, to meet Eleazer. In response to his request, Rebecca immediately led him to her family's home. He quickly gained Rebecca's mother's and brother Laban's approval after displaying his gifts of silver and gold jewelry along with bracelets and earrings made of precious metal.

Eleazer might, thus, have fallen asleep peacefully that night, satisfied that he had accomplished his arduous assignment easily; that he could return to his master the following morning and bring Rebecca with him, and that everything would proceed with unexpected speed. You can imagine his shock when Laban responded to the good man's request to send me away him by saying:

"But [the servant] said to them, Do not hinder and delay me seeing that the Lord has caused me to go prosperously on my way. Send me away, that I may go to my master." (Genesis 24:55)

Nobody but God is privy to Laban's potential motivation. However, I think his motivations were consistent with who he was as a person. It is safe to assume that everything in the background was responsible for his later behavior against Jacob. Eleazer's insistence was mostly made for Rebecca's benefit. She had expressed interest in his proposal.

"And they said, We will call the girl and ask her [what is] her desire." (Genesis 24:57).

And He was certain that Isaac would be a suitable husband for her. Anyone can imagine that Rebekah had a difficult time coming to the conclusion that she would have to live a nomadic life going forward. In spite of this, she willingly married Isaac after leaving everything she knew.

THE GIVER OF LOVE USUALLY SUFFERS THE MOST

Many people treat their own spouses with the utmost disregard. One will forgive their spouse if the former is disregarded and they often forget trivial details. But to disregard one's spouse or the person they live with is a bizarre folly and a serious sin.

Paul's preaching at Ephesus and elsewhere tended toward the practical. He did not withhold anything that would benefit them, and the greatest benefit he anticipated they would gain from his sharing the full counsel of God was that they should conduct themselves in the manner expressed below:

"...each man of you [without exception] love his wife as [being in a sense] his very own self; and let the wife see that she respects and reverences her husband [f]that she notices him, regards him, honors him, prefers him, venerates, and esteems him; and [g]that she defers to him, praises him, and loves and admires him exceedingly]" (Ephesians 5:33).

The husband and wife are not to be separated except by death. He is to govern her, but with a love-infused authority. In Genesis, Moses makes it clear that marriage is exclusive and irrevocable. God proved the exclusivity that was implied by creating just one woman. Malachi shares that viewpoint and says:

"Yet you ask, Why does He reject it? Because the Lord was witness [to the covenant made at your marriage] between you and the wife of your youth, against whom you have dealt treacherously and to whom you were faithless. Yet she is your companion and the wife of your covenant [made by your marriage vows]. And did not God make [you and your wife] one [flesh]? Did not One make you and preserve your spirit alive? And why [did God make you two] one? Because He sought a godly offspring [from your union]. Therefore take heed to yourselves, and let no one deal treacherously and be faithless to the wife of his youth." (Malachi 2:14-15).

Paul infers meaning from Adam's comments about Eve and makes a point about the importance of those loving feelings without which there is a risk that the husband's rule could turn into a heavy yoke.

"Then Adam said, This [creature] is now bone of my bones and flesh of my flesh;" (Genesis 2:23).

Thus, Paul writes:

"Husbands, love your wives, as Christ loved the church and gave Himself up for her, So that He might sanctify her, having cleansed her

by the washing of water with the Word, That He might present the church to Himself in glorious splendor, without spot or wrinkle or any such things [that she might be holy and faultless]. Even so husbands should love their wives as [being in a sense] their own bodies. He who loves his own wife loves himself. For no man ever hated his own flesh, but nourishes and carefully protects and cherishes it, as Christ does the church, Because we are members (parts) of His body. For this reason a man shall leave his father and his mother and shall be joined to his wife, and the two shall become one flesh." (Ephesians 5: 25-31)

Although Paul's letter to the Ephesians offers more instruction than the book of Genesis, Moses' instructions are, nevertheless, explicitly mentioned along with their adoption and expansion. Paul clearly references Adam, saying: *"This is now bone of my bones and flesh of my flesh". (Genesis 2:23a)*

In addition, the phrases, which express the union of the husband and wife on purpose, are stated in a way that provides a commentary highlighting their significance. In Genesis 2:24, Adam asserts:

"Therefore a man shall leave his father and his mother and shall become united and cleave to his wife, and they shall become one flesh"

In Ephesians, Paul asserts: "They two shall be one flesh." Thus, he clarifies for his audience that unity cannot be expanded to include more than two people. A marriage is between a man and a woman, not between a man and several women or between several men and one woman.

Paul has done nothing more than our Blessed Lord Himself in adding that. Paul referenced passages from the gospels of Matthew and Mark. The full oneness does not appear to permit a multiplicity of wives both conceptually and from history. It is difficult to understand how it can accept the separation of the marriage.

History reveals the following as the major contributors to the degrading treatment of women: forced marriage, polygamy, including concubinage, confinement (which was a result of the first two), slavery of captured women (which was closely related to concubinage), and divorce. Any type of polygamy robs women of their rightful status and limits their influence in the home. History has shown that polygamy ends the husband's love and affection or, more precisely, prevents its growth because of rivalry. It causes conflict in the family. It is a very fertile ground for competition, insults, bickering, etc.

The oldest type of divorce, arbitrary divorce, effectively turns women into slaves by giving their husbands all control over them. When a man throws his wife out of the house and offers her little or no support, she loses her relationship with her children. A man could not be more absolute than given the power of life and death.

The Universal Command

In the beginning, the relations of woman to man, by the words "Increase and multiply", God created Adam and Eve as the representatives of the next generation and as mirrors of themselves. God had already seen the limitations of Adam alone. He couldn't create his race by himself. Then, God provided a woman to serve as his wife.

Adam, therefore, produced his race through and through his wife. It does clarify that without Eve, Adam would not have been able to have children who would be reflections of himself. Therefore, the man and the woman are in charge of bringing forth new human beings. Putting aside the responsibility of procreation, a woman also contributes to a man's life in other significant ways. She serves as his subordinate, helpmeet, friend, helper, confidante, and counselor. She is all of those things because her nature is the ideal complement to his. The characteristics of the guy fit the woman and place her in her other relationships.

Additionally, it demonstrates that a woman was never meant to be a man's slave; that is incompatible with, at least, her two other relationships. (Matthew 19:5; Mark 10:8).

Submission to someone is not the same as being a slave to them. The superior has the right to rule over the subordinate for the benefit of the whole community and, ultimately, of both parties. Our consciences inform us that it is right from the outset for the weak to submit to the stronger.

"Wives, be subject (be submissive and adapt yourselves) to your own husbands as [a service] to the Lord." (Ephesians 5:22).

He is your husband, your leader, and your friend; submit to him. Why does this advice matter?

We do well to understand an instruction by its interpretation and functionality: the functionality and interpretation, in this case, is "as [a service] to the Lord." Therefore, the submission here meant is ultimate to God.

The interpretation holds that the fighting spirit in many people, particularly women, indicates that they have not submitted to God: obsessing, envy, rivalry, anger, and resentment are all signs that the heart is not submissive but, instead, it is still ferociously self-willed and defiant.

Lack of submission is not a novel or uncommon human flaw; it has been the source of all sin since the fall in the Garden of Eden. Since our mother, Eve, reached out to take the forbidden fruit and her husband followed her in pitting the human will against the divine, the sons of men have all been guilty of disobedience to God's will.

Adam and Eve made their own decisions and refused to submit their wills to God's commandments. Thus, their offspring have thought independently ever since; they refuse to submit their reasoning to God. The Eve-like women are earth-loving and will not submit their affections. The Adam-like men want to set their own laws and be their own masters.

It is apparent that many women who are irate, haughty, argumentative, and selfish lack submission. Some women find the concept of submission repulsive in and of itself. They refuse to submit to anyone and, instead, want to rule as their own gods and law. The word "submit" irritates them. If, for any reason, they have a higher rank in society than their husbands, they murmur in their hearts, *"Who is my husband that I should submit to."* That is abhorrent since we did not create ourselves.

"Know (perceive, recongnize, and understand with approval) that the Lord is God! It is He Who has made us, not we ourselves [and we are His]! We are His people and the sheep of His pasture." (Psalm 100:3).

God should and will be superior to all other humans because it is His will that determines whether we will or not. Many people talk about the rights of man, especially in America, but we should also consider God's rights. Because His rights are the foundation of all other rights and are the world's first, highest, most certain, most solemn rights. God's absolute and unalienable right over the creatures He created is that:

"Wives, be subject (be submissive and adapt yourselves) to your own husbands as [a service] to the Lord." (Ephesians 5:22).

The primary purpose of the master's authority over the slave is to serve the master's interests; however, the slave's interests must also be considered. In practice, men frequently act in accordance with an idea and overlook the interests of the slave, which is the complete submission of one person to another for the sole advantage of that other person. This idea is expressed in some interpretations. However, no human authority can be unrestricted; it must always be constrained by divine law. This applies to all forms of authority, including husbands, priests, presidents, etc. However, the authority held for the benefit of all is significantly different from authority held for the profit of the holder alone.

If it is not more correct to say that the misuse of power by many in positions of authority has been the only thing that has been demonstrated, then it has always been a vice of those in positions of power not to use their authority at all. Since God is so kind, so wise, and so full of loving thoughtfulness, it must always be in a husband's best interest to submit to God for his wife to easily submit to him in the Lord and prevent a collision of wills.

The Submitting Wife Has Rights

Everyone who cares agrees that something needs to be done to promote marriage and family. Everyone acknowledges that the fundamentals of marriage, family, church, and state are deteriorating. And while many people acknowledge it, they also offer solutions for improvement, treatment, and correction; many of which are fruitless.

If you pay attention, I will repeat some of the measures the book of Genesis suggests being undertaken to bring about the proper relationship between a husband and a wife. God, through Moses, outlined three responsibilities for the wife: companionship, help, and obedience. In relation to those obligations or duties, man has three rights. These rights have corresponding duties or obligations just like all other rights. If the wife is the husband's companion, the husband must be hers and fulfill the duty to establish the privilege. If a woman serves as a man's helpmeet, she is entitled to both the compensation that is due to her as his companion and a provision from the earnings from their shared labor. If a man is in charge of a woman, he should display restraint, kindness, and affection while doing so. All of those obligations and rights are resolved into the unity of the husband and wife, which upholds the obligations and imposes restrictions on the rights. The relationship, which consists of three aspects with a specific relationship to each other, is susceptible to perversion by overemphasizing or disregarding any of them or by introducing new principles. It has been twisted in all three of those ways.

The Ruling Husband Has Rights

While talking to Jesus Christ, the centurion said:

"For I also am a man subject to authority, with soldiers subject to me. (Matthew 8:9 KJV).

Some commentators have attempted to change the centurion's meaning by claiming that he was saying:

"I am under authority, simply a subaltern officer, and yet I can do so-and-so."

The centurion, however, meant that he was a man under authority, not just a private person but Caesar's servant. He was recognizable by his costume as a member of one of the Roman legions, and the insignia on his regimentals indicated that he was a centurion — a leader who got his authority and position from the great Emperor in Rome. He was "a man under authority."

In a similar vein, the Bible teaches that wherever there is authority, men should rule, and women should submit to them. God established marriage and appointed the man to carry out the role of a leader, giving him the higher authority and the power to do so. Therefore, a man has a woman under him, just as a centurion has soldiers under him.

In a relationship as close as a marriage, subordination appears necessary to grow kind emotions and Love. Respectful use of authority and peaceful acceptance of subordination foster the growth of Love, where rivalry is the most hazardous element. If there had been a tenth as much Love as there had been wealth, many marriages would have been extremely heaven on earth.

It is so amazing that Love often chooses to knock on the isolated cottage door of the destitute woman, illuminating their home with pleasure, rather than unwinding on the plush sofas of the palace of great monarchs. A superior may therefore feel intense Love for an inferior much like a mother feels for her child. As a child does for its parent, an inferior may feel intense affection for a superior. Gratitude is among the lowest and weakest characteristics of humanity.

To reciprocate Love is a human-like act. However, it is widely agreed that one of the lowest character flaws is to return hatred for Love. Even a dog perceives benefits from a human as showing Love. The animal tries to show its appreciation for the person by becoming attached to them in every way possible. *"The ox knows his owner, and the ass his master's crib."* A relationship with a lot of

Love can lessen the use of power, yet the kind use of power seems to improve the relationship.

When there is no rivalry, no claim to power, and no need for it to be used, Love may exist amongst equals; nonetheless, rivalry and fights over authority kill Love.

God could have established the institution of marriage with just a man and no woman or with just a woman and no man. However, He was happy to approve of marriage between a man and a woman. What a lovely thing that God would choose to engage the two! Therefore, a husband or a wife or a man or a woman who chooses to follow only some of the laws governing the institution of marriage while disobeying others undermines this tenet and exposes the flimsy institution to unwarranted storms.

The superior in the institution of marriage should ensure that Love is far superior to the usual run of Love — when those loves are not bound to time and the norm but instead, stretch to eternity and bless the soul; when loves are of such weight that they overwhelm the recipient; gratitude and submission would surely surface when Love is so powerful that it overwhelms the recipient since the benefit is so enormous.

Mutual And Collective Responsibilties Make A Good Marriage

The general principle of the institution of marriage and the universe of God is that through living for the benefit of others, we will also benefit ourselves. When family and community members do not push one another but, instead, go on their own paths, it is an extraordinarily great blessing. There are several worker categories, and they all need to work collectively.

Alas! There are often conflicts among members of the family and the community. What is even worse is workers in communities may not always be as amicable with one another, and some may even have a cold attitude toward others who don't do the same kind of work as they. On the other hand, God designed men and women to cooperate in marriage by carrying out various tasks.

God has given each sex its own set of fields and distinct bodily, mental, and moral constitutions suited to each field. A man and a woman were created to participate in life's activities, one in a role that the other was less suited for. This entails a diversity that gives the thoughts and passions more room to operate. The two sexes coexist in societies that are each a unit; even yet, specific men and women are joined to each other through marriage, making them one.

The average person does not notice Abraham's faithful wife because he is the only character in the faith story. But God does not pass by. Our God never forgets the good public in the dark. In His concern for the bigger, God does not ignore the smaller. Both Sarah and her husband, Abraham, were guarded by God throughout their lives.

Sarah was, in life, covered with the shield of God, as well as Abraham, her husband: she shared the same tomb with Abraham when he died and was buried, and she now has the same delight in heaven and a similar record in the Bible.

"After this, Abraham buried Sarah his wife in the cave of the field of Machpelah to the east of Mamre, that is, Hebron, in the land of Canaan. The field and the cave in it were conveyed to Abraham for a permanent burial place by the sons of Heth." (Genesis 23:19-20)

God is able to produce excellent items on a tiny scale. Similar to how rare pearls and precious stones are seldom found in vast amounts of rock but rather only inside a restricted scope, the most beautiful and valuable virtues are typically found in the most modest people. A person can be too big to be excellent but never too small to be courteous; therefore, examine the superior character of Abraham. God says:

"Look to Abraham your father and to Sarah who bore you; for I called him when he was but one, and I blessed him and made him many." (Isaiah 51:2)

The lifespan of Sarah was 127 years. And it would be fair to say that she was married to Abraham for half of those years. However, neither Sarah nor Abraham transformed into each other over those years. Diversity in unity is the end goal. However, misunderstandings can arise due to diversity. God developed the idea of woman's submission to resolve these conflicts.

We can only fully understand the principles of patriarchal life after spending time with Abraham, Sarah's husband, among the flocks and in the tent with Sarah.

All For The Unity Of A Relationship

It is said that "the first law of heaven is order, and the second law of heaven is diversity".

This statement is unquestionably true in terms of Providence. God has manifested His grace in the history of humanity in the most astonishing diversity. God's grace has always been shown in the same way but has always operated in diverse ways. So, the general rule in the physical and moral universe is that unity in diversity is required for completion. Without subordination, true unity cannot be attained through vain repetition.

This rule applies to relationships between the sexes, as well as to relationships between men and women generally and between specific husbands and wives who are married. Both a woman and another person mimic men in a subservient manner. However, she is not "a milder man." A woman has a unique constitution; one whose components are similar to those found in a man's but it is introduced in varying quantities. While she is still a different kind of man who is unsuited for them, this matches her for her distinctive functions.

The similarities and differences between a man and a woman are many. Therefore, a woman is ideal to be a man's friend, supporter, and advisor. However, the same conditions that made her suitable for carrying out her assigned duties rendered her unsuitable for the man's. I could go on and on about all the minute details of what a woman means to a man, but it would be redundant given what I have just stated in the broad, straightforward overview.

When a woman is at her most captivating elements, she is simple but sweet. She has a strong, venerable charisma that mesmerizes her husband. Like a comforting breeze, her presence is melodic. The language of her heart is so filled with Love, faith, and enthusiasm for a heavenly hope that the passage of time does not weaken its power or take anything away from its natural, spontaneous freshness.

The Non-Violent Spirit Of A Woman

Women have inherently soft hearts; they know little about violence but love deeply. Their understanding of a situation may not always be completely developed, but their hearts are ablaze. As a result, it is sometimes asserted that because women are more loving than men, they more accurately reflect God's likeness because God is Love. The Bible declares that God is Love but does not state that this is all He is. The Bible should be studied and used in accordance with common sense, just like any other book.

No matter how thoroughly an author may have expressed themselves in their writing, if you took a few sentences here and there, you might force the author to say something he or she has never intended; or even persuade them to support viewpoints they loathe. So, it is with the Bible: if we ignore a passage's context and overall flow, we miss the mind of the Holy Spirit and, instead, insert our own thoughts into the words of the Holy Ghost rather than bringing forth the mind of God from them.

Like many others in the Bible, the sentence does not fully reflect the entirety of truth; rather, it must be compared to other passages which will restrict and modify its meaning. God is Love, but He is also Jealous, a God of Peace but a Man of War. His nature includes power, justice, wisdom, and Love, yet none of them supplants or supersedes the others. In some of these areas, men outperform women. In comparison to men, women do not entirely mirror God's likeness.

"For a man ought not to wear anything on his head [in church], for he is the image and [reflected] glory of God [his function of government reflects the majesty of the divine Rule]; but woman is [the expression of] man's glory (majesty, preeminence)." (1 Corinthians 11:7).

The union of the two natures of a man and a woman, however, more closely resembles the image of God than either of the sexes alone. That necessitates the dynamic and spiritual union that is created when a husband and a wife consummate their marriage.

A husband and a wife should evolve into unity through intimacy and mutual appreciation to the point where one appears to be the other's complementary quality, and the mention of one implies the other. The couple should walk in the Lord toward one goal at a time. They must coexist as one soul in two bodies without struggles. For this reason, a Christian must marry a fellow Christian; to provide room for the Holy Spirit to arouse a passionate longing for God's glory in the husband and a parallel passionate longing in the wife. The husband's food and drink then becomes his wife's and both then enter the same joys.

The significance of the marriage bond is profound - oh, for the grace to embody it in human similes! I will just state that this is something that can only be understood by the spiritual mind and should not be explained in human words at all.

I lack the proper language to communicate this truth; letters, syllables, and words fall short. I can only express the following: the relationship between a husband and a wife is the deepest, most vital, and also most mysterious. And if every spouse knew that, they would never consider getting a divorce.

CHAPTER 09

THE MYSTERY OF MARRIAGE

More often, the institution of marriage is not one of ancestry. It is covenanted between two individuals who may have been complete strangers in the early years of their life. Marriage is a chosen covenant, not a bond based on natural birth. It is not regulated by genealogy, and inequalities do not hinder it.

Except for the few months before their marriage, they may have hardly ever exchanged eye contact. It is possible that the two families might have never met before and that they lived on opposite sides of the world. The man might have been a wealthy American who is managing pieces of enormous property while the woman might have been penniless and living in a far-off African village.

A suitable bachelor, however, meets the requirements of a suitable bachelorette just like a glove fits a hand. That bachelor abroad desires a woman over there in a distant nation, and vice versa. He feels unfulfilled; he fantasizes about having a helpmeet; his passion tickles him like an adder; it burns within him like a fire that is constantly fed with a new fuel; but when he meets the woman he longs for, he encounters rest, and he says to himself: *"This is bone of bones and flesh of the flesh" (Genesis 2:23a).*

Before becoming married, a man and a woman are known to be two separate people with separate wills, interests, and capacities for all aspects of life. And after they get married, the husband-and-wife blend to become one flesh in lovely harmony, as if with glue or pitch, so that each is hidden and cannot be easily brought back into view. Now the glue that unites the husband and wife is Love, Unity, and Sanctity. They are, without a doubt, the enigmatic elements of marriage, and they are so intimately related that it's possible they are just two sides of the same coin.

All married couples concur that their relationship is mysterious, not trivial, but involves a huge mystery; unity and sanctity are the two things concealed inside themselves, so concealed that reason cannot have discovered them. They are all intimately related and add to the mystique surrounding marriage. The triune elements flow from unanimity once God has given it His blessing.

Although Paul specifically mentioned Jesus Christ and the Church in that context of mystery, it appears that he was referring to the entirety of the passage and possibly especially to the married couple's unity, which is a profound mystery.

Wrong Perception About Marriage

Marriage has strong claims on our attention as a matter of religious reflection since it is intimately interwoven with both the temporal and spiritual prosperity and pleasure of humanity. Since this union corresponds to the Marriage of the Lord and the Church, the state of one must always keep up with the state of the other due to their close relationship. Hence, the state of Marriage among Christians is always a gauge of the Church's own status.

But because of how poorly marriage is considered today by certain groups, neither the married relationship nor its communication is often considered in terms of spirituality or permanent existence. But the fact that the case and condition of marriage are what they are, it shouldn't be startling. Because when we consider how some Churches have actively promoted the conception that Concubinage is preferable to a state of marriage from a religious standpoint because it is more chaste and spiritual, it becomes clear how these Churches have contributed to giving marriage a carnal and earthly character.

However, I appreciate that many churches still uphold the truth of God's Word and have rightfully condemned a sizable percentage of the world populace that undermines the institution of marriage.

The world needs lone people who can stand tall amidst the sarcastic group and read the mysterious letter of Adam to his descendants about the mysterious relationship that:

"Then Adam said, this [creature] is now bone of my bones and flesh of my flesh; she shall be called Woman because she was taken out of a man." (Genesis 2:23).

And at the very close of the Old Testament, Malachi teaches the same lessons:

"Yet you ask, why does He reject it? Because the Lord was witness [to the covenant made at your marriage] between you and the wife of your youth, against whom you have dealt treacherously and to whom you were faithless. Yet she is your companion and the wife of your covenant [made by your marriage vows]. And did not God make [you and your wife] one [flesh]? Did not One make you and preserve your spirit alive? And why [did God make you two] one? Because He sought a godly offspring [from your union]. Therefore, take heed to yourselves, and let no one deal treacherously and be faithless to the wife of his youth." (Malachi 2:14-15).

The doctrine of Adam's letter is entirely incorporated into the New Testament. Jesus Christ repeatedly adopted it, and Matthew and Mark both recorded them. In His rebuttal to the Pharisees on divorce, Jesus Christ makes reference to this Genesis chapter and affirms its unique relevance to marriage. He stated:

"...Have you never read that He Who made them from the beginning made them male and female, And said, For this reason a man shall leave his father and mother and shall be united firmly (joined inseparably) to his wife, and the two shall become one flesh? So they are no longer two, but one flesh. What therefore God has joined together, let not man put asunder (separate)." (Matthew 19:4-6).

God clearly stated the origin and essence of marriage in the creation of man in the Bible.

"God said, Let Us [Father, Son and Holy Spirit] make mankind in Our image, after Our likeness." (2:26a)

GOD IS THE FOUNDATION OF MARRIAGE

All of those statements, when taken as a whole, indicate a fundamental truth: Man was created in God's likeness and image, which means that man possesses both infinite and finite qualities from the Divine nature. At creation, God gave man His fundamental nature. Every human is affected by this truth. Everyone starts with God. God is the source of the fundamental components that make up every human being, as well as our immaculate and pure character.

According to the universal laws of heredity, man receives all of his mental faculties and moral qualities from God just as every seed obtains its qualities from the plant that produced it, every animal receives its form and nature from its parents, and every child receives its nature from its parents. Jesus Christ taught us to pray to our Father thus:

"Pray, therefore, like this: Our Father Who is in heaven, hallowed (kept holy) be Your name." (Matthew 6:9)

And He did not instruct us to do that out of politeness or as an analogy; it is a declaration of a true fact.

The logical conclusion is that God is the source of both the affections and the intellectual powers which are the feminine and masculine aspects of man's character respectively. Every human being must possess these aspects of the human intellect which we can generally refer to as love and wisdom or goodness and truth. Either love or truth cannot define a human being by itself. The two characteristics or elements must be combined.

Truth gives love its shape and provides it with its means of action, while love gives truth all of its strength. Before any of these two fundamental components of the human mind can function, they must be united and married. The union formed through marriage is natural. It is comparable to the relationship between substance and form. Both the man and the woman merge into one, becoming one. So, that is where marriage originated. It originates with God. He is the source of it in its purest and finest form because He is the union of love and wisdom.

This does not imply that God's wisdom is the whole and proper embodiment of His love or that His wisdom best expresses His love in all its fullness and perfection. Similar to how human minds work, there is no excess of one over the other. As they move through the creation, they take on separate spiritual and material forms distinct from each other, each embodying the same fundamental components in varying degrees and being attracted to one another by force from their shared origin.

This power we call "attraction" is a term used to describe the ability of something or a person to draw in other people. Love is seductive in its nature. Like a trumpet, it draws people to hear a declaration. Love draws people in like a net does with fish. Due to the affinities between the particles of matter, they attract other homogenous particles to form new bodies when they merge, linked together, or get wedded.

Marriage transforms gases into solids and liquids like water and precious stones. The ocean continuously vents its steaming breaths into the sky without resentment. Instead of closing the doors to its rolling waves, it exposes all of its richness to the sun which then draws heavily from the royal coffers of the deep. However, the ocean is not lessened since all of the rivers work together to keep the sea full to the coast.

The clouds in the sky empty themselves of rain when they are full, but they do not disappear because "Following the rain, they return; "and the ocean below seems to be so happy to be feeding its sister ocean across the firmament on a constant basis. Therefore, the entire aquatic apparatus is kept in motion by each portion acting upon its next neighbor and the next upon the next, just as wheels with bands are made to operate together, and wheels with cogs work upon one another. Each wheel exerts a force on its neighbor, and their combined effect on one another results in compensation for the total. In this way, nature attracts everything to herself. All of the planets are drawn to the sun's fiery center.

Love Can Unite Two Souls Together

In addition, dualism exists throughout creation in both its most extreme and simplest forms. There are the passive and the active everywhere; things are made for one another and use one another in unity. They exhibit a marriage-like quality everywhere they are found and precisely embody male and female features. This universal principle creates unity in infinite variation by permeating everything, dividing everything, and uniting everything. The union of a man and a woman, called marriage, is merely the most notable manifestation of the universal marriage by which each is tied to the other and the other to the Lord.

Therefore, the combination of love and wisdom, good and truth, or unity and sanctity is the highest and most universal kind of marriage which has its roots in God.

Marriage has its roots in the very depths and foundations of a man's Spirit, in the very roots and foundations of his human nature. God created both male and female humans. As we have above–below, allow–forbid, argue–agree, arrest–free, arrival–departure, asleep–awake, attack–defend, bad–good, so and there is heat-cold, light-darkness, emotion-thought, the heart-the lungs, love-wisdom. God has, thus, united man and woman together. Therefore, God is the source of marriage, which manifests in man and woman as its highest, innermost, and most complete form.

Marriage is fundamentally the union of two minds or souls because it has its human origins in the fundamentals and most inward aspects of man's nature. The theme and setting of its action are the Human Spirit. Therefore, it has a spiritual nature. It is neither a civil nor a legal contract in and of itself, and religious endorsement has no bearing on it.

In the truest sense of the word, it is as impossible for the state or the Church to marry a man and a woman as it would be to unite light and heat or to mix two different types of material components.

Family members, the Church, and the State may impose restrictions on marriage for a variety of reasons. They may impose requirements and legal frameworks for its organic and obvious completion. The three divinely appointed institutions are free to defend and preserve marriage through the use of their authority as it is both their right and responsibility. However, none of the three institutions has the ability to either unify or divide human souls.

The Church may approve it and commemorate its completion through solemn ceremonies. The church's leadership and counselors may instruct the man and woman who enter the marriage bond regarding its nature, its goal, and the necessary steps that should be taken prior to it. However, its mission and authority are limited there. It is unable to affirm or break the inner, invisible links that unite souls; she cannot even touch them. Only God has the power to unite two human souls so that they become one.

This fact - that true marriage can only be affected by Him who created man male and female - will become more apparent if it is even remotely imaginable when we examine the nature of that power that connects man and woman and makes the two into one.

The force that binds a man and a woman together and unites their souls is love which is a spiritual attraction that functions in interior ways similar to the attraction between physical bodies. True marriage is influenced and sanctified by love. The degree and character of love and the level of a man's character in which marriage occurs define the marriage's degree and nature. That is a fundamental truth that significantly impacts the marriage as a whole.

Without some understanding of the different levels or degrees of the human mind, each of which has its unique faculties and attributes, it is sometimes impossible for anyone to understand the fundamental nature of marriage. Due to their ignorance of the inherently mysterious nature of marriage, many people mistakenly believe that sex is merely a physical differentiation and that marriage is only a temporary connection whose ties dissolve with the death of the physical body.

"…the combination of love and wisdom, good and truth, or unity and sanctity is the highest and most universal kind of marriage, which has its roots in God."

It's A Great Honor To Marry

Marriage has the highest level of sanctity; therefore, those who are conscious of it seek it out and work to preserve it. When they do find it, they do not lose interest in seeing that it develops in grace so that the fullest benefits of its blessing might be realized. Although the Bible makes reference to the sanctity of the married state, people almost universally reject the concept. Thankfully, marriage is always recognized as a hallowed institution in the true Church of God.

Among the early and many modern Christians, the solemnization of the union was and is affectionately referred to as the Holy Matrimony. However, the common understanding of the holy solemnization of marriage is that it simply denotes a superficial innocence and a kind of negative holiness. Simply said, many people believe that holiness is the antithesis of unholiness. Without a better understanding, people assume that unholiness is the same as sin; as a result, it has a type of positive connotation, with holiness acting as its negation. Therefore, holy matrimony comes to represent nothing more to such minds than the fact that marriage is not fornication.

God cannot be satisfied if people are persuaded to believe that marriage is an alternative to fornication. His goal is for every married couple to actually have the full meaning of:

"Let marriage be held in honor (Marriage is honorable in all, and the bed undefiled: but whoremongers and adulterers God will judge." (Hebrews 13:4) (Mark 10:3-9).

God wants marriage to be honorable; He also wants the bed in the marriage to be pure; and finally, God has threatened immorality with His judgment. The word "honorable" has a positive and affirmative connotation, implying some significant attribute that creates results and modifies the nature of deeds, rendering what would, otherwise, be blameless.

If the passage from the Epistle to the Hebrews was the only foundation for the sanctity of marriage, it would have to be more than the absence of sin. However, the Divine institution implies that it ought to be greater. It is the divinely preordained method by which man is to carry out a clear command. This is nothing less than holy. There is a verse in Isaiah that supports this viewpoint:

"If you turn away your foot from [traveling unduly on] the Sabbath, from doing your own pleasure on My holy day, and call the Sabbath a [spiritual delight, the holy day of the Lord honorable, and honor Him and it, etc. (Isaiah 58:13).

Marriage is honorable because it supports many of God's highest goals and contributes to society as a whole. Hence, God commits His sacred oracles to a husband and wife. Anyone who enters the Holy Matrimony according to God's ordinance is made honorable by that very fact.

Every human person receives a few stray glimmers of God's honor, but those who partake in the institution of marriage receive the highest honor to some extent. Theirs are the commands of honor engraved with the divine finger; theirs is a sacred and instructive ritual; and theirs is a line of priests of the marriage who have been appointed to enjoy God's favor.

Those who participate in the marriage institution are deemed honorable. A husband and a wife are honored by being selected for special duty for the procreation of the human race in conjunction with all special honors.

THE SACREDNESS OF MARRIAGE

The most treasured and intimate relationship that two people can have is to get married. And the sanctity of the marriage relationship transcends a simple innocence brought about by express permission such as that given after the COVID-19 pandemic, to remove masks. Many people who have attempted to look into the mystique of the sanctity of marriage have lost the eyes of their reason. It is a sanctity that bestows holiness on people and their behaviors. It is closely related to the other marriage - related components.

God created mankind, male and female, in order that they individually find someone to love outside of themselves, for their shared love to grow in each other's capacity to receive Divine life, and for their support of each other to bring them together as one. And throughout the Golden Age of humanity, they did unite through a process of orderly and harmonious progression.

As the unique characteristics of man and woman emerged, each one sent forth strands of thought and affection that were embraced. We should never stop marveling at the fact that a man and a woman may truly become one flesh. That any man or woman could merge into one of another kind is beyond amazing.

The blessing of God, which only comes to a relationship founded on an agreement to every aspect of Christian marriage and which also bestows unity and sanctity, is the source of the holiness of marriage. These mysterious ingredients give rise to useful elements.

The first-time marriage is mentioned in the Bible, and the reasons why it was established are explained in the following words:

"And Adam gave names to all the livestock and to the birds of the air and to every [wild] beast of the field; but for Adam there was not found a helper meet (suitable, adapted, complementary) for him." (Genesis 2:20)

Malachi, a prophet, reiterates the same concepts and makes the following connection between the sacredness of marriage and its inseparable unity:

"Yet you why does He reject it? ask, Because the Lord was witness [to the covenant made at your marriage] between you and the wife of your youth, against whom you have dealt treacherously and to whom you were faithless. Yet she is your companion and the wife of your covenant [made by your marriage vows]. And did not God make [you and your wife] one [flesh]? Did not One make you and preserve your spirit alive?

And why [did God make you two] one? Because He sought a godly offspring [from your union]. Therefore, take heed to yourselves, and let no one deal treacherously and be faithless to the wife of his youth. (Malachi 2:14-15).

This passage discusses the relationship between the Church and God. But in order to demonstrate that both were on the prophet's mind, a strong analogy is made between that relationship and marriage. This is also true of a passage from the previously mentioned Epistle to the Ephesians. Both Malachi and the apostle Paul simultaneously discussed both because they saw marriage as an appropriate metaphor for the relationship between God and the Church.

They both wrote as a consequence of divine inspiration. Because of its relationship to even more sacred concepts, the philosophy around marriage is stronger, not weaker. Additionally, the various angles from which Malachi and Paul approach the topic give their lessons more impact.

Malachi uses the relationship between a husband and wife as an example while discussing the relationship between God and His Church which was the nation of Israel. He switches between them in such a way that it is almost unclear which one he considers to be his main topic. Paul, whiles discussing the marital condition, uses the relationship between Jesus Christ and His Church as an analogy. In his writings, he also compares the relationship between God and the Church to that of a husband and wife, as if what applies to one also applies to the other.

Male And Female Marriage Is Akin To Christ's Marriage To The Church

The idea of the sanctity of marriage is most clearly declared in the New Testament:

"Wives, be subject (be submissive and adapt yourselves [a service] to the Lord". (Ephesians 5:22)

Apostle Paul makes reference to submitting as being necessary saying that wives must submit to their husbands as to the Lord. Just as the authority of the one great Head is the foundation for all lower headships, the divine fatherhood is the ground for every lower fatherhood, and each, in its place, is to be regarded as His shadow. As a result, the headship of the husband over his wife is a shadow of the headship of Jesus Christ over the Church, which clarifies the nature of the husband's authority.

The rule of Jesus Christ is a rule that works to the benefit of the ruled. The word "savior" is filled with associations of self-sacrificing love, and He rules the Church as Himself, her savior or deliverer from slavery. The same holds true for Christian husbands. But Jesus Christ is more than just the Church's Head. The idea of Jesus Christ as the Head of the Church takes on a new significance.

"But the person who is united to the Lord becomes one spirit with Him." (1 Corinthians 6:17).

We could even be said to be, like Eve from Adam, "of his flesh and of his bones" since we derive our life from his manhood. Jesus Christ is the husband of the Church in the fullest sense of the word.

Paul seems to use the analogy of three different marriage traditions to better define the relationship between Jesus Christ and the

Church. By paying a dowry, the husband first wins the object of her heart as his bride. After being purified in a bath, the bride is then made ready for her husband before being presented to him in bridal beauty. Therefore, Jesus Christ first "gave Himself for her" because He loved the Church. In another letter to the Ephesians, Paul described the Church as having been "purchased".

"You were bought with a price [purchased with a preciousness and paid for, made His own]. So then, honor God and bring glory to Him in your body." (1 Corinthians 6:20).

Thus, having won the Church as His bride, with the power of the word, Jesus Christ cleansed her in the water laver.

"That He might present the church to Himself in glorious splendor, without spot or wrinkle or any such things [that she might be holy and faultless]." (Ephesians 5:27).

The same apostle explicitly discusses the sanctifying effect of marriage in another epistle without making any particular mention of the unity of the husband and wife.

"To the rest I declare – I, not the Lord [for Jesus did not discuss this] – that if any brother has a wife who does not believe [in Christ] and she consents to live with him, he should not leave or divorce her." (1 Corinthians 7:12)

This verse appears to convey two doctrines: The first is the sanctifying force of marriage which sanctifies both the non-believing spouse and the children. Contrary to what some people believe and what has been stated above, this is not an opportunity to convert an unbeliever's husband or wife: (1 Peter 3:1) Paul, again, cites Peter and says:

"But to the married people I give charge - not I but the Lord - that the wife is not to separate from her husband." (1 Corinthians 7:10).

A Privilege To Be Desired

In one of Paul's many teachings on marriage, he also teaches another doctrine: that an unholy marriage can be made holy through the faith of a believing husband or wife, even if the other spouse in the union chooses to remain unbelieving.

Sometimes, a Christian must journey to heaven alone because God has chosen to remove them from the neighborhood of an ungodly family, and despite their example, prayers, and admonitions, the unbelievers in the family do not accept Jesus Christ. Because of this, the family's sole Christian continues their lonesome journey to the heavens as a speckled bird among them.

However, it happens much more often that the same God, who is the God of Abraham, also becomes the God of Sarah, Isaac, and ultimately Jacob.

Although regeneration is not based on blood or birth, the God of Hannah becomes the God of Samuel, and although grace does not run in families, it does often, nearly always, occur that God uses one member of a household to call the others to Himself. He extends an invitation to someone and then utilizes that person as a type of spiritual sham to attract the rest of the family into the gospel net.

Similar to those mentioned by Apostle Paul, the people he was referring to were converts who had already been married to non-Christians before converting.

There had been no Christian marriage, no agreement to one, and no petition or acceptance of divine approval. The marriage was not initially holy; it only became so after one of the participants converted to Christianity. The faith that brought about this shift had to be a vibrant faith that was motivated by love and resulted in a desire for God's blessing, as well as an agreement with the Christian view of marriage. The marriage was then made holy, both partners were made holy for the sake of the marriage, and the children were made holy.

Christians who feel they've been single too long and wish to wed an unbeliever should not use this situation as an excuse or a method to take advantage of the situation. Any Christian who decides to become a missionary to gain a soul through marriage will make a grave mistake. They must take caution as they might not find solace in Paul's doctrine under such conditions.

The Unequally Yoked, God Abhors

There is a very definite difference between a Christian and an unbeliever, just as there was between the Egyptians and the Israelites of the Bible. That dividing line has existed and will continue to exist forever. Every attempt to merge the serpent seed with the woman seed must fail. There will always be a significant difference between the Church and the world no matter how debased the Church may become or how transformed the world may become. God prohibits all of His children from marrying anyone who is not a child of His because He insists that distinction be maintained.

God often reminded the Israelites that they are special people and gave them the command to keep their distance from other people.

They were not to form alliances with the Canaanites or intermarry with them as mentioned here:

"For you are a holy people to the Lord your God; the Lord your God has chosen you to be a people for Himself, a special treasure above all the peoples on the face of the earth." (Deuteronomy 7:6 NKJV)

God's explanation is that:

"But because the Lord loves you and because He would keep the oath which He had sworn to your fathers, the Lord has brought you out with a mighty hand and redeemed you out of the house of bondage, from the hand of Pharaoh king of Egypt." (Deuteronomy 7:8).

By a unique and particular redemption by which Jesus Christ loved His Church and offered Himself for her, Christians are also redeemed from among men. Christians have moral commitments to come out of the world and to be separate from it since we were specially purchased with His precious blood.

"They are not of the world [worldly, belonging to the world), [just] as I am not of the world. (John 17:16).

Therefore, it may be appropriate to say that neither of those ideologies will support interfaith marriage in our world. Such a union was wicked at the beginning but, like other unlawful unions, may become lawful by the eventual faith and repentance of one of the partners. In the same Epistle, Paul describes widows in a way that applies to all Christians (1 Corinthians 7:39).

A man or a virgin's liberty cannot be greater than a widow's. In another scripture, marriage to an unbeliever is explicitly forbidden (2 Corinthians 6:14-18). Therefore, marriage to an unbeliever is immoral. It exposes the unequally yoked Christian to enormous temptations even if it is not explicitly sinful. Those who purposefully give in to temptation have little chance of receiving the blessing that is given to those who just continue a commitment they had entered into without knowledge of Christian law.

Such people are commanded by Paul to recognize the rights that the other party has accrued even though the newly converted Christian is still ignorant. Paul or Peter gives their blessing to the traditional excuse of getting married in order to win over the unbeliever. Both of them talk about staying married, not about purposefully getting married in an ungodly way. (1 Corinthians 7:39/2 Corinthians 6:14-15).

The Sanctity Of Marriage Is Of God

Most Christians firmly believe that before departing from this world, Jesus Christ established two ordinances: baptism and the Lord's Supper. His disciples maintained those ordinances throughout all ages and they will until the end of the world. All Christians, without exception, acknowledge the appointment to the two ordinances. This is due to the Community of Friends' steadfast adherence to the lofty ideals of the Holy Ghost baptism and the communion of the soul with Jesus Christ meant to be represented by the external and visible evidence despite other people's rejection of them (ordinances).

The acknowledgment of both the interior grace and the practice of the outward sign has been regarded by nearly all Christians throughout history as being a part of the will of Jesus Christ.

Christians have a similar dedication to the marriage ordinance, and I want to bring this to our open and serious notice.

The same principles that underlie all of Jesus Christ's commands, which He issued to every one of His disciples immediately before ascending to heaven, serve as the foundation for the ordinance of marriage. Better yet, He instituted a marriage ordinance that persisted throughout His earthly mission until His disciples took over from Him. This ordinance was given from the moment that the man and the woman were created.

All of Jesus Christ's and His apostles' statements concerning marriage demonstrate that it has a mystical sanctity. No one will dispute the sacrament status of marriage. It is "ordained by Jesus Christ" as a substantial affirmation and compelling illustration of God's good intentions for humanity, through which He works invisibly in us and serves to not only reawaken but also to consolidate and reaffirm our confidence in Him.

The husband and wife have had to travel together thus far. The fact that it is called "marriage" suggests that they agree with the vast majority of other Christians on, at least, one issue relating to the marriage ordinance. The marriage between the husband and wife should be regarded as a representation of the unity between Jesus Christ and His Church. Jesus' handling of the Church as His wife should serve as an example for husbands, and the Church's behavior should serve as an example for wives. Since type and antitype are related in such a way, it is difficult to imagine any assertion being made about one that is not also true, to some extent, of the other.

A Kind Of Unity Without Which A Marriage Will Not Survive

Every Marriage that God has approved unites God, man and woman. That marriage is always clearly a Trinity in One. And it appears that the sanctification that the Divine blessing bestows on the union is what gives such marriages their sanctity. This could be what makes up its irrevocable quality:

"What therefore God has joined together, let not man put asunder (separate)." (Matthew 19:6).

There is no prohibition against severing the ties that God has not established. The warning that man, who can only look at the outside appearance, cannot separate people who, in the apparent appearance, have been joined by God may need to be repeated throughout the book. Marriage's two mysterious components, unity and sanctity, should be seen as its core or the point of connection for all other elements whether they be causes or effects.

Theological terminology like "sanctification" has a much more limited meaning than what is found in the Bible. However, I do not intend to confuse anyone in its ever-expanding scope, so I made the decision to try less in the hopes of doing more tasks successfully. The word "sanctification" in the Bible has a considerably broader connotation than systematic divines give it. It is a well-known fact that the Old Testament often helps in our understanding of the New Testament while also explaining the Old.

Now, the word "sanctify" usually appears in the Old Testament and has three distinct meanings. In the Old Testament, the word "sanctify" typically refers to *setting apart*. It entails repurposing anything that was formerly common or might have properly been used for regular purposes solely for the benefit of God. The term, in its earliest use in the Bible, was related to God;

"And God blessed (spoke good of) the seventh day, set it apart as His own, and hallowed it, because on it God rested from all His work which He had created and done." (Genesis 2:3).

That day could have previously been a regular day, but God set it aside for His own use so that on the seventh day, man should not work for himself but rather, rest and worship his Creator.

On account of the destruction of Egypt's firstborn, God also claimed ownership of the firstborn of both humans and animals.

"Sanctify (consecrate, set apart) to Me all the firstborn [males]; whatever is first to open the womb among the Israelites, both of man and of beast, is Mine." (Exodus 13:2)

The tribe of Levi was chosen to serve as the firstborn and to stand before the Lord day and night in his tabernacle and temple; as a result, individuals chosen to serve as priests and Levites were considered to be sanctified (Leviticus 27:14).

Therefore, God declared in the most important passage of the Bible:

"And I will sanctify the Tent of Meeting and the altar;" (Exodus 29:44)

It is obvious enough that God intended for it to be set aside as His house, the unique location of His residence where the golden light of the Shekinah could shine out between the cherubim, the dazzling proof that the Lord God dwelt among His people. The following are examples that have the same impact.

The Old Testament plainly demonstrates that the word "sanctify" can sometimes signify nothing more than setting apart for sacred purposes. It explains how Jesus Christ described Himself in the New Testament:

"Say ye of him, whom the Father hath sanctified, and sent into the world, thou blaspheme; because I said, I am the Son of God?" (John 10: 36 KJV).

The term "sanctify" is sometimes translated as "consecrate" or "set apart" in the Amplified Bible

"[If that is true] do you say of the One Whom the Father consecrated and dedicated and set apart for Himself and sent into the world, You are blaspheming, because I said, I am the Son of God?" (John 10:36).

Thus, since Jesus Christ was sinless, He did not need to be cleaned. Because He was immaculately formed and gloriously preserved from any touch or taint of evil, He did not require the sanctifying work of the Spirit within Him to purge Him of dross or corruption.

Jesus Christ is set apart is what is relayed in the text. In another notable and well-known passage in the gospel, Jesus speaks about His disciples:

"And so for their sake and on their behalf I sanctify (dedicate, consecrate) Myself, that they also may be sanctified (dedicated, consecrated, made holy) in the Truth." (John 17:19).

Once more, Jesus Christ just intended to convey that He committed Himself entirely to God's service and focused solely on His Father's business.

Every marriage that has been divinely sanctioned and those who have committed their life to it are, therefore, totally sanctified. They are legally separated from others by the marriage ordinance, and they are clearly and obviously separated from others by the Spirit of Marriage.

Let's put the doctrine aside for a moment and consider it in practice. A vessel, a cup, an altar, or a tool was never used for ordinary uses again after it had been set aside for divine worship. The only person who may consume the golden cup is the priest. Therefore, the family's priest, who also happens to be the husband, has the authority to sip from the marriage's cup.

God's bare laver was not intended for routine personal hygiene; the altar should not be taken lightly. Even the altar's tongs and the light snuffers were forbidden from being used for any kind of shared purpose. What a somber and suggestive fact this is! If God sanctifies a husband and a wife through the institution of marriage, they should never be utilized for anything other than God.

A wife just exclaimed, "What?" "Not for us?" Your body is not your own; it belongs to your husband, and vice versa.

"For the wife does not have [exclusive] authority and control over her own body, but the husband [has his rights]; likewise also the husband does not have [exclusive] authority and control over body, but the wife [has her rights] (1 Corinthians 7:4).

Undoubtedly, a husband and wife must continue to work hard at being beneficial to themselves, the family, the Church, and the society. They ought to serve God sincerely:

"So then, whether you eat or drink, or whatever you may do, do all for the honor and glory of God." (1 Corinthians 10:31).

A husband and a wife are not an ordinary couple any more than the altar was common. It is just as great a sacrilege for them to live for themselves or according to their own will as if they could have profaned the most sacred place, utilized the holy fire for their own kitchen, censered for everyday scent or candlestick for their own bedroom.

God owns marriage in its entirety; therefore, anyone who attempts to appropriate it without intending to set themselves apart refrains from doing so. The agreement could be compared to the root from which unity and sanctity sprout when they are nurtured by divine grace. The practical characteristics such as exclusivity, indissolubleness, and the husband's power are the outcomes of unity and sanctity. The irrevocable nature of marriage has already been demonstrated to be linked to the highest authority's unity.

The incompatibility of polygamy with unity and its consequent exclusivity is obvious to the mere human understanding.

One Of The Best Decisions Toward Marrying

Marriage is not a thing merely tolerated or licensed. It is a duty under the ordinary circumstances of mankind. This is implied in the Divine declaration that "It is not good for man to be alone"; which was the assignment of the Divine motive for creating woman and instituting marriage.

Paul has been supposed to contradict this Divine motive.

"My desire is to have you free from all anxiety and distressing care. The unmarried man is anxious about the things of the Lord how he may please the Lord;" (1 Corinthians 7:32).

Paul explicitly states that he was speaking in reference to the current difficulties. He was expressing his opinion on whether it was appropriate for Christians to get married in those days. The question of whether the people were more likely to be better single Christians than married was put to Paul. He responded to this delicate subject with extraordinary tact and faithfulness.

And in doing so, he established a significant general concept that is far more valuable to the Church today than Paul's individual viewpoint on the subject of marriage or non-marriage.

Paul claimed he received no instructions from the Lord regarding virgins but instead, offered his opinion as someone who had received the Lord's mercy by being faithful: In this instance, he did not speak as a result of divine inspiration; rather, he did so as an experienced and dedicated man offering his opinion for the benefit of others and the great task that was so dear to him. Paul's statements are, by no means, to be disregarded in that context.

Paul was discussing Christian marriage in this instance, and he initially advised Christians to put off getting married since His reasons are found in the following scripture as state earlier.

"My desire is to have you free from all anxiety and distressing care. The unmarried man is anxious about the things of the Lord how he may please the Lord;" (1 Corinthians 7:32).

The state of events that prompted Paul to offer his advice was essential. There were periods of intense persecution. Christians were routinely hauled before judges, subjected to lions in an amphitheater, imprisoned, or given horrible executions; in such situations, a few people would want family around.

If it was appropriate, the Christian man without a wife or a child might flee in an instant. He also did not need to consider it when he was standing before Herod or any of the Roman governors: *"If I die, who will take care of my wife and fatherless children?"*

When the single man put on his headgear, he housed his entire family, allowing him to travel about to preach the gospel or flee persecution without having to go through the trouble of transferring a family from one place to another. Paul desired for the Church to be like an army that was not burdened with baggage because the historical context required that they be unburdened much like soldiers on death marches.

Paul traveled with only a little amount of canvas covering all of his possessions, along with a couple of tools and a reel of thread that he used to construct tents wherever he went. He was, therefore, careless.

Being single in those difficult and desperate times was the finest thing a man or woman could do since it put them in the best possible position for escape, suffering, service, or death. Because it was not a time when people could settle down, work in trade, or engage in agriculture, Paul advised against getting married at that time. However, in general, no one nowadays is able to speak as Paul did. I have said before that the Bible does not address every individual moral dilemma that might develop or provide a solution to every action-related issue. Because the situation is clearly distinct, we should adhere to the broad concept rather than the specific example made by Paul.

There are several passages in which Paul sees marriage as a women's responsibility in normal circumstances, which shows that this is essentially his meaning. And if it is a woman's responsibility, it is almost certainly a male responsibility as well. Paul provided instructions for widows.

"So I would have younger [widows] marry, bear children, guide the household, [and] not give opponents of the faith occasion for slander or reproach." (1 Timothy 5:14).

Paul also suggests in other writings that marriage is a woman's natural and rightful state. Let' hear him:

"Bid the older women similarly to be reverent and devout in their deportment as becomes those engaged in sacred service, not slanderers or slaves to drink. They are to give good counsel and be teachers of what is right and noble, So that they will wisely train the young women to be – sane and sober of mind (temperate, disciplined) and to love their husbands and their children, To be self-controlled, chaste, homemakers, good-natured (kindhearted), adapting and subordinating themselves to their husbands, that the word of God may not be exposed to reproach (blasphemed or discredited)" (Titus 2:3-5).

The Genesis verse and his theology can be made to agree if we assume that they both mean something along these lines: It is not good for a man to be alone; it is better for him to have suitable help. However, it is better for him to be alone than to have a companion who is not a help or who is not suitable for him, whether due to flaws in her character or other factors that make it unsuitable for him to marry. It has happened that women who were single and suffering a lot of care felt comfort, love, and care after being married and coming under their husband's protection. Overall, they served God better and were less cautious in the marital estate; therefore, it was best for them in the truest sense. This standard of serving God freely should be used while making decisions on marriage.

However, many singles never judge in this manner at all. So, for a variety of reasons other than love, many men and women have hurried into marriage. Many may be well aware that those marriages would result in all kinds of worry and trouble and prevent them from being able to do anything for God, yet they entered into it.

Overall, it is possible to say that marriage is a Divine institution into which God normally intends for men and women to enter. The rule is susceptible to various exceptions, some more common than others, depending on the social setting and stage of life. However, marriage is the divinely appointed state of man, and not only is it free from sin, but it also has a significant element of holiness - possibly the most important ingredient - conformity to the will of God.

This makes the institution so pleasing to God that He has given it the ability to sanctify all that is associated with it. However, the consequences of the divine blessing - including sanctity and all the others - are not bestowed upon unions that violate the divine law.

I will, thus, give forth the fundamental principle that every Christian man and woman must adopt - *"I would have you to be free from cares."* You must acknowledge that you are purchased with a price and that you do not really belong to yourself. And for everything, including marriage-related issues, you are to seek God's will and ask the following question:

"Will being married or single makes it easier for me to honor God? I can only hope and pray that getting married won't make me so wary that it prevents me from serving God".

There is much to be said on each side, but may I fervently pray that the scales be tipped in my favor so that I may truly serve Jesus Christ in the state of matrimony. If so, I am free to participate in the marriage; if not, I am not supposed to indulge my own desires at Jesus' expense. I would forfeit my salvation in order to get married. Therefore, if being single and going to heaven were preferable to getting married and losing my salvation, one should choose to stay single.

Since we are not yet at our full potential, we cannot afford to lose everything that we already possess. No, we must completely surrender to Jesus Christ, keeping in mind Paul's exhortation in the following words:

"My desire is to have you free from all anxiety and distressing care. The unmarried man is anxious about the things of the Lord how he may please the Lord;" (1 Corinthians 7:32).

"...if being single and going to heaven were preferable to getting married and losing my salvation, one should choose to stay single."

THE MYSTERY OF BECOMING ONE FLESH (1)

We usually hear about unity among married couples, but I sincerely doubt that many of them truly understand what it entails. Unfortunately, many husbands and wives have very little personal knowledge of unity in marriage. To explain the unity between a husband and wife, various hypotheses have been proposed. One is the concept that the husband and wife have a mystical connection that unites them and turns them into one flesh during sexual activity. It was once acknowledged by human laws as being necessary for a marriage to be complete, and it continues to have some influence on people's opinions. Other issues may arise as a result, for which this is not the appropriate forum.

That theory may be related to a unique passage from Paul's writings which could have been used to support the claim that Adam spoke inspired words upon the introduction of his wife but was kept here due to its other message. Let's hear that:

> "But if the unbelieving partner [actually] leaves, let him do so; in such [cases the remaining brother or sister is not morally bound. But God has called us to peace. For, wife, how can you be sure of converting and saving your husband? Husband, how can you be sure of converting and saving your wife? Only, let each one [seek to conduct himself and regulate his affairs so as to] lead the life which the Lord has allotted and imparted to him and to which God has invited and summoned him. This is my order in all the churches." (1 Corinthians 7:15-17)

Paul seems to believe that even though it is against the law, sexual activity has the ability to make two people become one flesh. The passage is complex; it, definitely, teaches that fornication makes the fornicators into one flesh in a certain sense, but it is likely not required to think that the union is irrevocable.

Men's having many wives is not unheard of, and some cultural traditions and world religions even endorse the practice. Many men and women will have had sexual relations with more than 100 persons by the time they leave this world.

Zsa Zsa Gabor married nine different men. Elizabeth Taylor married eight times to seven different men. Larry King married eight times to seven different women. However, hearing about a woman who has multiple marriages strikes me as strange. A form of polygamy known as polyandry occurs when a woman simultaneously marries two or more men. Contrary to God's command, familial polyandry, in which two or more brothers are married to the same wife and the wife has equal "sexual access" to them, is a practice in many parts of the world.

CHINA

Fraternal polyandry is a common practice among the people of Tibet and Nepal, parts of China and India respectively. Its foundation is the idea that a child can have more than one Father and that when two or more brothers marry the same woman, they, usually, all have equal access to her sexually. If the family is destitute and unable to distribute their property among the children of several fathers, the practice is encouraged. Therefore, they marry the same woman in order to maintain their large homes and little farmlands.

KENYA

In August 2013, Kenyans reported a polygamous union between two men and the woman they both loved. Notably, polyandry is not expressly prohibited under Kenyan law, and those who engage in it are not subject to punishment. The Kenyan Massai ethnic group has also been linked to polyandry cases.

NIGERIA

There are tribes in Nigeria that permit polyandry despite the practice being mostly uncommon there. The Irigwe people of Northern Nigeria have a custom of giving women multiple husbands, or "co-husbands. "In Nigeria, the Irigwe people practiced co-marriage until their council decided to forbid it in 1968. Up until that point, women lived in different homes with different husbands, and the children's paternity was determined by the husband whose house the woman was residing in at the time.

INDIA

There are many tribes in India that practice polyandry. While polyandry is common among Paharis in some areas of North India, particularly in the Jaunsarbawar district, a minority of Kinnauri residents justify and engage in polyandry. Five brothers, who were descended from the Pachi Pandavas, married Draupadi, the daughter of King Panchala. They considered it necessary to continue the custom. In addition to them, polyandry is also practiced by the Toda tribe of the Nilgris, the Najanad Vellala of Travancor e, and several Nair caste systems in South India. 13 percent of the 753 Tibetan families surveyed by Tibet University in 1988 engaged in polyandry.

SOUTH AMERICA

Polyandry was practiced by tribes in South America as well; the Bororo did it, and up to 70% of Amazonian civilizations may have approved of multiple fathers. Fraternal polyandry is also practiced by the Tupi-Kawahib. Let's now presume that all of these marriages are irrevocable unions because the man and the woman have become one flesh through sexual activity. If so, there is a lot of polygamy and polyandry in the world. They cannot be; since God has not joined the fornicators, they may be separated.

What many people call marriage is rarely a marriage where a man and a woman did not intend to get married, make a pact to live together in line with God's law, and ask for, expect, or receive divine blessing. Fornication, which is an act of sin, cannot have received a divine blessing, and a marriage cannot be united or holy without a divine blessing. Even though the sin does not result in an irrevocable Christian marriage, it may, nonetheless, have some mystical power to bring the sinners together in a mysterious unity of guilt. A Christian's guilt is shameful and an insult to God. By the sin of those who failed to seek the blessing of God, it may become a curse in many ways.

The Mystery Of Becoming One Flesh (2)

Nobody will ever understand how a man and a woman can be two separate individual fleshes, yet one flesh. For my part, I have long since given up trying to understand this enormous mystery because God must, by definition, be unfathomable given everything He does.

I envision a plethora of philosophers presenting their diverse hypotheses regarding the mystique of the union of a husband and a wife, some of which are as brilliant as the noonday. One of those theories holds that love induces unity in marriage. By "love", they mean the romantic feeling that prompts marriage and often, though not always, leads to sexual arousal between lovers.

Everything that is filled with love has the ability to reflect, radiate, and receive. Therefore, I am unable to provide you with every phrase that can be used to define love since they are amazing words and wonderful theories that we could discuss till thy kingdom come.

The emotion that underlies that theory of marital unity is made up of a self-love-derived passion and generous love. Marriage causes the passion to diminish and the love to grow into romantic love. While it may be beneficial to feel that way before getting married, that emotion cannot unite a marriage. It is impossible to give in to such feelings. It is the seed of marital affection, but like many seeds, it may not grow into the fruit, or the fruit may ripen and die.

Any couple who subscribes to that theory and bases their marriage exclusively on feelings is guaranteed to believe their marriage may dissolve ten days after the honeymoon. Love that originates from emotions and is only expressed through feelings burns like a fig leaf very quickly before it goes out. With such love, a person may appear to only love their spouse intermittently when they are aroused or during special events.

However, it's crucial for husbands and wives to understand that when you choose your spouse, you adopt them into your life for a lifetime. And the love that will keep each other alive in that life and unite married couples together is a deep-seated and enduring love. Such love is comparable to the flames burning inside a volcano. Although it may not always erupt, there is always a fierce heat inside. And when it is needed, it erupts, spewing rivers of heaving, seething, boiling, and burning molten. Even when things are fairly quiet and still, the married couple's hearts must constantly be burning with passion.

Therefore, husbands, have a strong, placid, compassionate, and well-founded love for your wives. Because wives love a lot, I would have avoided telling them to behave similarly. However, there is no graduation from a love college. So, wives, keep loving your husbands as if you cannot possibly love anyone or anything else. Spouses, while you can use little letters to spell out all other names, use the biggest capital letters to express your love for your spouse. Love each other fervently, without any boundaries. Because if you do not, the marriage's pleasures can pass as quickly as they arrive. The love in the marriage may become fleeting and anything but intense causing frames and feelings to shift and preventing a husband and wife from remaining united.

May God the Father, who gives the gift of marriage to humanity, establish the loving potential and capacity for His children to receive love in every marriage.

*"Love that originates from emotions and is only
expressed through feelings burns like
a fig leaf very quickly before it goes out."*

Sex May Be A Pivot In Marriage

Sex is one of the major topics of debate that has, for many years, surrounded the sanctity and mystique of the union in marriage. A controversy has developed around "Sex" which, when seen properly, is beneficial and healthy for marriage and may greatly benefit marital couples. However, misunderstandings have developed for two reasons. Some people have entirely disregarded all other facets of the institution of marriage and made "Sex" the main emphasis of marriage. Others have taken the institution too far and completely ignored "Sex" as something that is extremely trivial to the existence of the married institution. There is reason to worry that those disagreements, which have put the divine institution, purity, and utility at odds, would taint all pure spiritual love from which it derives the entirety of its purity and blessing.

People who place the highest value on sexual intimacy in marriage believe that this is what truly unites the husband and wife together. It is extremely likely to be, thus, considered in a purely human manner of thinking in the order of nature, yet in the order of grace, it is not.

Sexual relation passion and the union of a husband and a wife are closely related. Sexual relation passion is not a component of marriage despite the fact that it is intimately related to both the mysterious and the formative components. It is made the core of marriage in certain widely accepted theories of marriage that are related to the romantic notion of the relationship between the sexes. According to those theories, it encourages consent, unites the couples, precedes the marriage in the form of a seed, and in some ways, sanctifies the union. It takes on its full proportions after marriage and becomes unity by itself.

Such unity is not mystical in any way; it is just a conscious emotion that unites the wills of the married couple. That is passion between spouses, but it is not the mysterious connection that turns two people into one flesh. From the day of marriage's consummation *till death do them part*, much of the married couple's happiness depends on their sexual desire. However, it is not absolutely essential to marriage.

Romantic love does not always last forever; so; such an idea would conflict with the irrevocable character of marriage. The absence of romance and sexual relations, whether it formerly existed or not, is harmful to the married couple's short-term and dangerous to their long-term happiness. Without it, it is quite probable that the holy state's obligations will go unfulfilled or will be carried out carelessly and inadequately. The absence of sex in a marriage can have several negative effects: hatred can take the place of love, disrespect may take the place of respect, honor may give way to dishonor, fidelity may give way to infidelity, and sanctity could be replaced by adultery.

The absence of sex in a marriage that is occasionally brought on by illness, distance, or even an intentional act may be exceedingly harmful to the husband and wife. It does not, however, end the marriage as it would if sexual passion were its core principle. But I must stress that sexual union is necessary for the comfort and security of the marriage institution.

I support romantic marriage, and everyone who supports it deserves praise. It is challenging to give in to people who believe that a Christian marriage might be characterized as the beginning of righteous sexual passion because Christian doctrine forbids such emotion before marriage.

"The absence of romance and sexual relations, whether it formerly existed or not, is harmful to the married couple's short-term and dangerous to their long-term happiness."

Marriage Stabilizes The Human Soul

Human nature was undivided and united before man sinned, but the fall damaged this unity. Thus, sin is miscommunication, misunderstanding, and turmoil, and when it entered the world, it caused a separation between God and humans as well as miscommunication within the human heart. A normal average individual hears many voices, imaginations, and ideas simultaneously in a few seconds.

In the little garden of our nature, our reasons and our lusts fight with one another resulting in conflict and strife. There is a constant and obvious conflict between our conscience and our affections. Like Eve in the Garden of Eden, affection is the root of all evil in our nature. In the same way that Adam followed Eve, so too would our conscience have desired to do, but our newly awakened consciousness leads us to approve of what is good.

Our affection usually follows what is pleasant, but our conscience warns the mind of its foolishness; as a result, there is a conflict between the two powers of the soul. The affections want what the reason would reject, the will insists on what the judgment would renounce, and the lusts and passions both crave things that the intellect forbids.

A mutiny has broken out on board the ship of our humanity, and those forces that ought to be subordinates are vying for control. Two opposing forces pull us in different directions: the conscience pulls us in one direction, and the affections pull us in the other.

One of the safeguards that God has provided for humans to help stabilize the human soul is marriage.

"One of the safeguards that God has provided for humans to help stabilize the human soul is marriage."

Man And Woman Are The Embodiment Of Love And Wisdom

When we carefully consider the evidence of the Bible regarding the creation of man and woman, we will be able to learn that the distinction between the two sexes has a much higher origin and exists for a much greater purpose.

"So God created man in His own image, in the image and likeness of God He created him; male and female He created them." (Genesis 1:27).

Even though I've already talked about how both men and women are included in the term "man" and how they were made in God's image, it's vital to mention it again to clarify the bigger picture. Here, I want us to dig for the Divine image in both of them together rather than just in each one alone. Every human being, regardless of our gender, is similarly an image of God; nevertheless, when it comes to a particular aspect of His Divine essence, each male and each female are more specifically images of God. What do I mean by the distinction in the Divine nature that gave rise to and is the inverse of the division between sexes then?

The nature essence of God is made up of the two concepts of LOVE and WISDOM. Because God is Love and Wisdom in one, He created man to be a conduit for His love and wisdom. Therefore, man has two separate faculties for receiving life from God: a will to receive His love and an understanding to receive His wisdom. Without a doubt, both males and females have will and understanding since without either, neither would be considered human. However, they do not have either to the same degree which is a key factor in how they differ from each other.

In the masculine mind, understanding prevails over will, whereas in the feminine mind, will prevails over understanding. Since the mind takes its fundamental characteristics from its dominant or most active power, the male mind is predominantly intellect, and the female mind is primarily will. The difference between the two is that the woman is known for her strength of affection while the male is known for his analytical character. Therefore, there is a difference between men and women, and that is comparable to the difference between understanding and will. And as those were made to make one mind, they were also created to produce one man.

Their differences mirror those between love and wisdom for which the faculties of will and intellect were created; the woman was created to be a form of love and the man to be a form of wisdom. Humans' ability to acquire wisdom sets us apart from animals; and wisdom itself is what elevates him above them. However, unlike animals that act instinctively to maintain life without instruction, humans do not have the same instincts as animals. We can only learn the most basic concepts - including the fundamental necessities of life - through experience, imitation, and instruction.

Thus, man cannot develop wisdom without the inspiration of some form of love, specifically THE LOVE OF LEARNING TO AQUIRE WISDOM. The ability to acquire wisdom is the fundamental love that underlies all human development and endows mankind with the capacity for unending advancement. The need for knowledge, which is so intense even in childhood, shows it in its earliest stages of growth. The value of spiritual knowledge, especially the knowledge of God's will, cannot be overstated. A great scholar is somebody who has had the grace of God permeated knowledge into their mind, heart, and entire being.

Before any reasonable thought may appear, God, Himself, places the desire for His knowledge in His child's mind. And the fact that it has been so is a proof that it is a genuine act of inspiration from God designed to entice His children to Himself.

When we first become Christians, we typically do not feel the spiritual love of wisdom. It starts out, though, as a simple and beautiful illustration of God's love. When we revert to our childlike state and are prepared to learn from our heavenly Father in the wisdom from Him, we first start to feel the true love of which is the seed. However, after someone has grown wise and loves that wisdom within themselves out of their love of growing wise, they develop another love for themselves that we refer to as the LOVE OF WISDOM in order to separate it from the first.

However, because this is a man's love of his own wisdom, it is also known as intellectual pride or self-conceit. The male human being would be destroyed if such love persisted since it would react against the former and turn his wisdom into foolishness. Therefore, God predetermined from the beginning of time that this latter love would be extracted from the man and planted in the woman to achieve a spiritual marriage and bring about man's integrity.

So, God took the man's love of his own wisdom, which is the rib, his intellectual proprium or self-hood, and transformed it into a woman making her his bone and flesh. This lovely act of creative wisdom has changed what would have become the most self-centered and degrading love in man into the object of the most unselfish and uplifting affection. God purposely designed it this way so that the man's wisdom would also continue to be loved, and he would continue to be loved for his wisdom — but not by himself, but by someone more precious to him than himself, whose love would continue to have a predisposition toward improvement and happiness.

God created it in such a way that the woman will be kept in the single love, the love of the man's wisdom, and that the man will be preserved in the single love, the love of growing wise. From this, they derive their ability and propensity to reunite so that they once more become, as it were, one man. A man's wisdom and a woman's love, therefore, become superior to knowledge alone.

His knowledge, combined with her love, when used appropriately, equals wisdom.

While his knowledge may allow for foolishness, her love envelops it and drives it out. His knowledge serves as a Mercedes Benz, and her love drives. If this point of view is embraced, it will become clear that sex is fundamentally spiritual and, hence, eternal because it is rooted in the very structure of the human soul.

UNITY AND SANCTITY NURTURE SEXUAL ACTIVITY

The institution of marriage and its sanctity and unity are the sources, not the results, of sexual desire and its activities. The union of love and wisdom in God is marriage's initial and ultimate source. Creation, itself, was born out of this divine union, for everything in the universe was made by God out of divine love and divine wisdom.

One could argue that since many married people do not enjoy a sexual passion for the aforementioned reasons, marriage cannot be the cause of sexual passion. The assertion is unquestionably true, yet the inference does not follow.

There are many marriages that are entirely external; the legal requirements for marriage have been met, but not in the correct way. There has not been any sanctity, spiritual unity, or blessing from God. It should not come as a shock that there is little intimacy in sexual encounters under those conditions. If marriage is seen to be merely a civil contract, it cannot result in this kind of intimacy.

It also cannot arise from coexistence. It might help in its development by giving opportunities to see the endearing qualities of the object of affection. However, it cannot help the development because it can only reveal unlikable characteristics. The truth is that sexual love is a divine institution and that it belongs to the order of grace, at least, in its highest perfection.

Marriage is not a sacrament in which the recipient receives a special Divine grace pertaining to their salvation. However, it is a Divine institution whose blessing must be requested through prayer and will be granted to those who do so with the proper attitude and spirit. The institution is made holy by the Divine blessing which unites the people. In marriage, nature manifests itself in love and exhibits a unification of spirit and life.

All of this is exceedingly mysterious, but so are all of God's grace's workings. He upholds what He blesses on a daily basis through His Spirit. He who made them both male and female also maintained their unity. Each member of the marriage institution is required to partake in communion.

The microcosm of the human body may serve as an illustration of the unity of marriage. The entire human system depends on giving to survive. Blood does not enter the body's heart to be stored; instead, it is pumped through one valve and out through another. All of the liquids in a healthy body are perpetually in a condition of expenditure, just like the blood which never stops still anywhere. Therefore, unity and sanctity are the true causes of marriage rather than sexual activity.

Marriage's unity and sanctity are inextricably linked; neither could possibly exist without the other. Sexual relation pleasure will seldom be lacking where they are and hardly be found where they are not.

"And may the God of peace Him sanctify you through and through [separate you from profane things, make you pure and wholly consecrated to God]; and may our spirit and soul and body be preserved

sound and complete [and found] blameless at the coming of our Lord Jesus Christ (the Messiah). (1 Thessalonians 5:23).

"Marriage's unity and sanctity are inextricably linked; neither could possibly exist without the other."

MARRIAGE THRIVES ON THE REGENERATED NATURE OF MAN

Loving people are thoughtful and considerate. Thoughtful people who are affectionate and considerate are, yet people of godly people. Humans are something more than a body. We are triple-natured, composite beings, with our essence divided into three components: "spirit", "soul", and "body". However, there is a dual nature of the "body" and "soul" even in unregenerate people; thus, those who are not Christians.

The ideal state of a perfect human being is the composition of the spirit, soul, and body. The only sources of their "spirit" are their relationship with Jesus Christ as regenerate, sanctified people and the presence of the Holy Ghost within them.

Now, depending on whether a person is a Christian or not, this two- or three-part constitution is almost always brought up when talking about our human constitution.

"And may the God of peace Him sanctify you through and through [separate you from profane things, make you pure and wholly consecrated to God]; and may our spirit and soul and body be preserved sound and complete [and found] blameless at the coming of our Lord Jesus Christ (the Messiah)." (1 Thessalonians 5:23).

There are, thus, in a sense, three natures in every man and woman: the animal which corresponds to the body; the intellectual, also known as the soul which includes the faculties by which the intellect operates and the emotions by which it is aroused; and the moral, which is the spirit in which the emotions and faculties are under the control of the conscience and are compelled to recognize the difference between right and wrong.

The new nature superinduced by the Holy Spirit's indwelling overrides all of them in the regenerate and sanctified man sanctifying the other three with His own new nature. Marriage is intended for this configuration of men and women, and it is possible to think of it as having multiple sides that are tailored to the various facets of this complicated nature.

The "Body", "Soul", and "Spirit" present a genuine, albeit insufficient and flaw-ridden, understanding of the matter. Marriage has an animal element to it, one that caters to the desires of the animal nature. *"Surely, I am more brutish than any man." (Proverbs 30:2).*

Additionally, it has an intellectual aspect, or more precisely, two cognitively related sides. One of them, which is tailored to the requirements of the kind affection, is what is referred to as the emotional side. The other is associated with the faculties for which it offers work and help. It also has a moral component because it promotes the development of moral character. Therefore, marriage has four aspects, each of which is tied to a particular aspect of human nature.

Every Christian marriage has a fifth side known as the spiritual side which is equivalent to the spiritual nature to what the moral nature is to the moral nature. Marriage also possesses something that, if nothing else, may be considered a sixth side. The sixth is related to human-society relationships, making it intellectual. It is also related to the needs of animals, making them animals.

The rational side of marriage could be a reasonable name for it. Marriage's union, which is at its core, is related to the first five of these, and in a limited way, to the sixth. In a sense, the sanctity of marriage has relationships with the first four sides, but its unique relationship is with the fifth. In the truest sense, it is a part of the higher nature that has superinduced itself upon others through the action of divine force through the consenting human will.

To Make A Marriage Work, Everything Matters

Marriage is one of life's greatest mysteries. It is kept hidden from those who want to destroy its foundation but made very clear to those who want to uphold its institution.

The mystery of marriage is completely unknown to the majority of humanity. Unfortunately, not everyone who is supposed to see it does so. Through the lenses of societal perception, they could only dimly perceive it. The mystery of marriage is still veiled in a deeper sense unless the Holy Spirit has personally revealed it to each of us.

Marriage's sweetness and mystery are what render a person's spouse sufficient on their own. They cannot be replaced. It is a "mystery". Therefore, its sanctity is in the sanctification of the consent, the unity, and all of their results, as well as of all the faculties, feelings, instincts, and functions that are associated with marriage. Thus, every Christian marriage's unity and sanctity are inextricably linked and make up its core. However, the Holy Spirit's indwelling in the hearts of a husband and a wife produces a higher sanctity which is also true of their sanctification.

This elevates romantic love to the status of a holy virtue. Every work of sanctification in the hearts of men is the work of the Holy Ghost, yet because He is a Gentleman, He does not work against the will of a person or a couple.

For Good Marriage Decisions, Jesus Must Be The Reference Point

I will conclude this chapter by stating that Jesus Christ is the central figure in the marriage mystery. The concept of marriage comes from Him and is astonishingly heavenly in nature. Therefore, if someone wants to understand the concept of marriage, they must look at it from all angles rather than just one. They must analyze it through the eyes of Jesus who is love.

Marriage should not be entered into only on the basis of the emotions associated with one of the six ideologies. The majority of people concur that marriage has both animal and human sides to it although they do so more on a theoretical than on a practical basis.

Men, at least, marry for animal motives while women marry simply for human reasons. Such marriages are unhealthy and predisposed to failure. The marriages commonly referred to as "love matches" and are the product of emotional impulses are not any better even though many potential spouses tend to believe that those are the only suitable marriages. When we are considering marriage, no facet of it should be scorned or ignored. Nobody should get married without carefully weighing all the pros and cons. If a marriage is to be sanctified, all motivations for getting married or marrying a particular person must be kept in check with moral and religious principles.

CHAPTER 10

THE EDEN'S GARDEN

The human heart is a little garden; despite its invisibility, it harbors the thoughts and affections of a person's soul.

When considering Adam and Eve in the Garden, the first idea that comes to mind is related to the name "Eden". It is a Hebrew phrase that denotes joy or contentment. When taken into consideration, the Bible often uses the word "garden" to indicate a person's spiritual knowledge'.

"…And you shall be like a watered garden and like a spring of water whose waters fail not." (Isaiah 58:11).

It also implies the mental state in which a person easily understands and accepts spiritual concepts. Given that this peculiar mental state is referenced as a garden, compared to a garden, or simply referred to as a garden, we have no trouble concluding that the Garden of Eden represented man's spiritually intelligent state of love and happiness at the beginning of the world.

"And the Daughter of Zion [Jerusalem] is left like a [deserted] booth in a vineyard, like a lodge in a garden of cucumbers, like a besieged city [spared, but in the midst of desolation]". Isaiah 1:8

In Eden, Adam and Eve were spiritually sound. Their mental abilities did outpace those of the rest. Additionally, their sexual inclinations did not dominate their thought processes. The couple, therefore, offered God their innocent worship. Their being was harmoniously balanced, and all of their abilities were flawless. Adam and Eve were exactly as God had intended them to be in every way because that was how God had created them. Adam's nature was in perfect order much as a flawless vehicle that has just left the manufacturers' hands functions in concert with every part and submits to the mainspring at the center.

THE SYMBOLISM OF EDEN'S GARDEN

There are many intriguing aspects to the Garden of Eden, but I will only mention a few. It was planted east of Eden. In religious symbology, God is said to be in the East. We are looking spiritually eastward when we turn to God. One of Adam's and Eve's greatest blessings in the Garden of Eden was their FELLOWSHIP with God. God communed with Adam as he walked through the Garden much like a man converses with a friend. Given that God was the focus of Adam and Eve's religious beliefs, it was, therefore, assumed that the Garden of Eden was planted in Eden facing east.

God was the source of the couple's love, innocence, joy, and contentment. They rejoiced in being identified as belonging to God and having God's vitality pouring through them. Adam's and Eve's love and spiritual joy are symbolized by the Garden of Eden which also stands for their spiritual wisdom and knowledge.

There is a river that emerged from Eden to irrigate the Garden. A river could not physically flow out of Eden to irrigate the Garden. Although it was impossible in the natural world, it was attainable spiritually. The river represents wisdom as it is believed to be entering the mind from the source of wisdom which is God. The love of spiritual things in the intellect and the joy in pursuing them are the sources of the spirit of wisdom whose fountainhead is God. If a person does not have a passion and a desire to pursue wisdom, they cannot ever become wise.

Thus, the river of wisdom sprung from love and its joy gushed forth from Eden. It then set out to irrigate the Garden or to revive and enliven the human mind. The mysterious river, according to the Bible, was divided into four heads, watered Havilah, Ethiopia, Assyria, and the Euphrates - bordering nation.

> *"Now a river went out of Eden to water the garden; and from there it divided and became four [river] heads. The first is named Pishon; it is the one flowing around the whole land of Havilah, where there is gold" (Genesis 2:10-11).*

The human mind has four areas where reason and intellect can have an impact - the frontal lobe, the Parietal lobe, the Temporal lobe, and the Occipital lobe.

Frontal lobe: The Frontal lobe represents the will. It is situated near the front of the brain. It is that which is engaged in daily planning and self-management. This covers problem-solving, advanced planning, and emotional regulation. Also, it assists in phonation, word understanding, memory consolidation, and physical movement.

Parietal lobe: The parietal lobe represents rationality. It is located in the middle of the brain; assists in object identification and spatial awareness — it tells us where we are in relation to the things around us. It interprets touch and pain throughout the body.

Temporal lobe: This portion of the cerebral cortex represents the memory of the brain. It is located on the sides of the brain. While the right temporal lobe controls visual memory and language understanding, the left temporal lobe controls the processing of sight and sound.

Occipital lob: The occipital lobe represents understanding. It is situated at the rear of the brain and assists in decoding visual information by processing images and sending them back to your eyes. It enables a person to discern between object shapes and distances between them.

The four components of the brain - will, understanding, rationality, and memory - are spiritual domains that belong to the mind, not the physical world. Thus, when Adam and his wife sinned, and God drove them out of Eden, they lost more than just a physical Garden - they also lost a spiritual garden. They lost Eden which is a sacred symbol of love and all the benefits it brings. They lost their spiritual intelligence along with all the benefits that come with having it. In fact, Adam and Eve traded their spiritual life for a natural one. All of their order of nature was turned upside down. Sin caused the separation of the couple's natural and spiritual worlds. Since they no longer had God as their source of growth and no other means of growth, Adam and Eve both became spiritually dead. They turned into lifeless bodies with no ability to talk, hear, taste, smell, or respond to a call.

Even though God's voice was incredibly loving, Adam and Eve were unable to hear the love in it because they were spiritually dead; hence, they fled.

"But the Lord God called to Adam and said to him, Where are you? He said, I heard the sound of You [walking] in the garden, and I was afraid because I was naked; and I hid myself." (Genesis 3:9-10).

Being spiritually dead, the couple lacked power and, sadly, fellowship with God and even with themselves, leading them to live each other's lives entirely for themselves. Because Adam served as the federal head and representative of the entire human race, we were susceptible to the terrible effects of his fall. After the fall, Humanity became utterly selfish and turned their attention exclusively inward. We, also, evaluated how much we valued others based on what we could gain from them.

God created the universe in such a way that selfishness is the gravest imaginable violation of His law. Because of how He created the world, following His will means living for and serving others. God paved the safest path for us to pursue our own happiness while looking out for one another. However, due to the fall which imbued our nature with everything untrue and bad, man and woman became spiritually estranged from each other.

Despite being a garden by nature, the human heart and soul hardly deserve an appellation. Since the fall of man, it has been fully covered by weeds, including briars of covetousness, envy, deadly fornication, jealousy, and ungratefulness. There are no sweet fruits, only grapes of lies and apples of betrayal: what is supposed to be God's Garden has transformed into this revolting forest of growing wickedness. But lo, it is a dense wilderness filled with all kinds of infuriating things; it, also, bears abuse from thorns of cruelty and needles of inhumanity.

I see trees, but they drip with self-centeredness. I see another tree which flows with hatred and drips with murder. The death of the spiritual life severed the highest and most potent sources of the unifying power between the male and female. And many of the essentially natural tendencies toward oneness were corrupted as a result. The fall left the Garden of the Soul looking terribly unkempt.

THE PLOUGHER OF OUR SOUL

What kind of heavenly gardening may be applied to the Garden of the human soul to bring it back from the brink of drought conditions? It must be turned over by God, the great Farmer, in His own way. God cuts down all human goodly cedars, pleasures, and pride in order to prepare the heart to receive the good seed of the word later on just as a wise farmer does before sowing the seeds and having preparations for a harvest.

God sends out a rough plough of conviction to plow through the soul's Garden. He allows the surface to be broken up, the goobers to be segmented, the weeds to be eliminated, and the trash to be burned up by the fire.

Sometimes, through the power of His Spirit, God so severely harrows, crosses, and ploughs the soul that is almost brought to despair. God exterminates the soul's delicious sins so that it can no longer enjoy them and instead desires to be free of them. God does all these things to the Garden of the Soul to make it worthy of His ownership.

God sends out His messenger to sow a seed in the soul's Garden after the depressions, eggs, and soil have been cleared away. By the mouths of those messengers, the Holy Spirit gently plants the seed of God's Word and attends to it with the same tenderness. He also plants seeds from the heavenly nurseries which bear leaves from the Tree of Life.

As the soul hears the word of God, the seed of the word sprouts. The Garden of the Soul, which in the past could hardly be called a garden fit for Jesus Christ, develops buds, blossoms, and bear fruits that Jesus Christ will accept: love, joy, peace, patience, forbearance, kindness, goodness, faithfulness, gentleness, self-control, hope, and zeal. Any passerby who pays close attention notices that the Garden belongs to Jesus.

"The human heart is a little garden; despite its invisibility, it harbors the thoughts and affections of a person's soul."

THE WOMAN'S CONVERSION OF THE MAN'S LOVE

As mysterious as marriage is, it also serves as a ministry dedicated to winning souls. And the Bible says: *"…And he who wins souls is wise"* (Proverbs 11:30 NKJV).

Before I continue, I must respectfully say that I am not suggesting that Christian men and women should seek out and win over unbelievers so that they might be their spouses. The Bible categorically prohibits such an "unequally yoked" union.

"Do not be unequally yoked with unbelievers [do not make mismated alliances with them or come under a different yoke with them, inconsistent with your faith]. For what partnership have right living and right standing with God with iniquity and lawlessness? Or how can light have fellowship with darkness?" (2 Corinthians 6:14).

A wise person wouldn't do that because soul-winners have never been fools. The person Solomon, the wisest man, is referring to being wise even in ordinary circumstances to be able to accomplish such a supernatural feat through grace.

Now, the soul winner I am alluding to in the institution of marriage is the person who God qualifies to win souls by whatever other means Providence may assign them. When it comes to winning souls through the institution of marriage, the person doing it is typically someone who could have done anything else if God had been so-called. As I have already indicated, marriage is one of the safeguards God has created to stabilize the human soul.

Many factors that had the potential to separate man and woman have now been reconciled by that supernatural act of God on the soul. God, through Jesus Christ, has restored many outward links that bind men and women together. Men and women are now drawn to one another throughout history in every state and at every age. While Satan has done much to impede and repel man and woman, Jesus Christ has enabled humanity to work together to overcome obstacles to our regeneration. Therefore, man and woman can now support each other in overcoming life's difficulties and restoring the interior union and perfection of the state from which they were expelled.

It is safe to argue that every marriage between a man and a woman, even in the low and flawed forms in which it exists, is meant to help the husband and the wife in putting away their natural faults and falsities and help them to the development of a truly spiritual life. The love of one's self and the love of the world are the main barriers to human rebirth.

God created the woman, as I mentioned in the last chapter, in order that she converts the man's love for himself into his love for her. Therefore, the demise of marriage in terms of spiritual culture and soul victory is the suppression of or submission of self-love. The woman's conversion of the man accomplishes this goal in a variety of ways and serves as one of the most beautiful illustrations of how

Jesus Christ meets the needs of every human being and uses the same methods to foster the development of their spiritual nature, prevent them from straying further, and restore them to harmony with both the life of God and their fellow humans. Therefore, it is not incorrect to say that every bachelor and every bachelorette who desire to marry are unbelievers who yearn to be converted to the institution of marriage.

God always chooses the most appropriate means for the task at hand. When Abimelech was about to approach the entrance of the tower at Thebez to fire it, God prompted an unnamed woman to direct her to hurl an upper millstone in Abimelech's direction.

"But a certain woman cast an upper millstone [down] upon Abimelech's head and broke his skull" (Judges 9:53).

It was because the only weapon capable of striking a wicked Abimelech was a millstone. That was a man who, in order to rule, betrayed his own family and murdered 70 of his siblings. And since the unnamed woman was skilled in cooking, the millstone was the best weapon she could have used. God always adapts the instruments He uses to bring about the desired outcome, and in the marriage ministry, He uses the woman's soul to convert the man's spirit. There is no question that a husband and a wife who succeed in marriage in a godly way are neither simpletons nor fools since converting a love just like a soul in marriage is not a simple process.

Even though arrogant wiseacres might call a spouse who practices the godly marital ordinance dumb, they are the ones that God makes wise for Himself.

"…And he who wins souls is wise" (Proverbs 11: 30 NKJV).

Such people God makes wise for Himself though vainglorious wiseacres may dub them fools. Every woman who wins a man's love chooses a wise object. What could possibly be wiser than to honor God, and what could possibly be wiser than to truly bless our fellow human beings. It is a joyful thing for a woman to liberate a man's love from the gaping chasm, to hoist it up to the glorifying heaven, to free his love from Satan's tyranny, and to lead him into the freedom of Jesus Christ.

Any couple who reaches that level of superabundant love - those who can perceive spiritual reality with the same clarity that they perceive natural truth - is in Eden.

"God always adapts the instruments He uses to bring about the desired outcome, and in the marriage ministry, He uses the woman's soul to convert the man's spirit."

PARTIAL RETURN TO THE ERA OF INNOCENCE (THROUGH THE KNOWLEDGE OF CHRIST)

Adam's punishment for disobeying God's commandment to abstain from eating the forbidden fruit was that:

"In the sweat of your face shall you eat bread until you return to the ground, for out of it you were taken; for dust you are and to dust you shall return" (Genesis 3:19).

And God said to Eve:

> "To the woman He said, I will greatly multiply your grief and your suffering in pregnancy and the pangs of childbearing; with spasms of distress you will bring forth children. Yet your desire and craving will be for your husband, and he will rule over you" (Genesis 3:16).

Thus, it is evident that three factors contributed to Adam's and his wife's contentment in their original state: INNOCENCE, the incapacity to tell the difference between human and divine will in operation; EMPLOYMENT without exertion; without difficult or demanding work; EXEMPTION FROM SORROW or mental suffering.

In the strictest sense, human total Innocence can never be restored. There is no hope of ever bringing back Eden on earth by reverting to moral ignorance or insensibility because moral knowledge of good and evil never goes away, not even when someone becomes a Christian. It is irrevocable. It inevitably passes down from Adam and Eve to their descendants in every generation. Upon entering the world, everyone experiences a sense of lost Innocence.

"Behold, I was brought forth in [a state of] iniquity; my mother was sinful who conceived me [and I too am sinful]". (Psalm 51:5).

Therefore, we only gain control of our minds after someone brings a saving knowledge of Jesus Christ. And God commands us to apply that knowledge in a godly manner.

"See, I have set before you this day life and good, and death and evil." (Deuteronomy 30:15).

Every Christian couple, as well as every human, faces the challenge of returning to Eden through the knowledge of Jesus Christ, renouncing sin and choosing virtue. Thus, it is improbable that there won't be many difficulties between a husband and a wife's perfect spiritual connection.

Only Jesus Christ and, through Him, genuine Innocence can restore an unfertilized conscience of the husband and the wife in Eden.

Partial Return To The Era Of Innocence (Through Self-Sacrifice)

A fully developed man and a woman who were raised in separate households and under very dissimilar circumstances must have developed diverse habits and tastes; they are inclined to approach many issues from different, if not opposing, perspectives.

Before a unity of a man and a woman's interior lives can be established in outer activity, many things that have been second nature must also be placed on hold, adjusted, and given up. The first thing that commonly causes a hiccup in the smooth running of a husband and a wife's marriage is their different tastes and habits. The popularity of self-love extends even to devout Christians. Even when it does not demand it, it always feels that it deserves to be satisfied.

All of us are susceptible to self-love; while we take pleasure in the relaxing cordiality, we watch out that it isn't referred to as self-love. Christians religiously abhor self-love if it is so-called; if it is called anything else, we consume it as readily as an ox consumes water. If self-love remains dormant, there will be some benefits because progress is made when self-aggrandizement is even a little controlled.

If it gives in to another's admiration, it begins the most challenging process of rebirth. The commencement of this work is very well suited to the first stage of marriage. The newlyweds shower each other with many flawless perfect things.

The rich imagination of the husband and the wife bestows an atmosphere of sparkle upon every valued item. It highlights qualities, ignores flaws, and covers everything in its own shades. The characteristics that will yield fruit are maturing in this ideal existence. It is a lovely prognostication of joys that can appear along life's journey as the fundamental character is formed, becoming brighter and purer as the spiritual and godly levels of the mind open up.

The husband and the wife who mistakenly believe certain flowers to be the fruit (love, peace, patience, kindness, goodness, faithfulness, joy and self-control) are undoubtedly disappointed when the flowers wilt and drop. However, this very impression diverts attention away from actual problems, and masks thought and behavior patterns causing items of common interest in different household setups and numerous future goals to become consuming. As a result, the bonds between husband and wife grow stronger as others weaken, and the threads, that will unite them as one, are beginning to develop.

Without taking away from their flavor and vibrant color, they may sort each with its type and hedge them around with the tying growth of family ties. They may allow the bright hopes and expectations that rose up wild and chaotic in their early imaginations to live around their houses. So, even from the start of a marriage, the circumstances are ideal for addressing the specific needs and challenges of married life.

A husband and a wife might avoid this interaction and miss out the rich gifts which are the rough instruments that bring those fanciful hues of marriage, the rose-colored and wonderful hopes pouring from the opening fountain of life, and anything other than the stern and harsh and unyielding reality.

All of life's commitments and connections are governed by the same law. If we knew all the obstacles ahead of time, we would never succeed in achieving the goal we hold in the highest regard. But when the different habits, peculiarities of taste, and opposing viewpoints start to emerge through the receding mists of youthful fancy, a lot of shared hopes and worries are developed. There are a lot of ongoing activities in which the husband and the wife are both interested, and many pleasant memories continue to linger like the scent of flowers.

If they look to the future, they cannot help but see that their contentment depends on their shared patience and helpfulness, and a very strong incentive is provided for them to give up their own preferences and adapt to each other's customs and tastes.

Through God's wisdom and love, a husband and a wife can yield to the need and find satisfaction in it. When a husband and a wife have genuine, unselfish love for each other, this sacrificing of oneself for the benefit of the other will be gratifying and natural. The greater the outside variety of tastes and habits are, the greater the opportunity to demonstrate strength and depth of commitment. In the desire for a husband and a wife to live entirely for each other, the self will be forgotten.

In this case, regeneration is successful, and the husband and wife are introduced to the biggest and most important responsibility of their lives without suffering or conflict, even using joyful techniques.

In order to achieve the original purpose for which they were created, the husband and wife begin offering support. They support each other in becoming whatever their most brilliant imaginations have ever imagined and unimaginably more.

Idolatry, A Sign Of The Fall Of Humanity

Since the fall, humanity has become a profoundly carnal and an unspiritual creature. After the fall, humanity became soul and soil after lying on the ground for a very long time. The earth, however, badly pollutes our souls! As a result, our soul blends with the soil. Satan, then, enslaved us to a life of idolatry. Even those who have experienced a rebirth and a new nature, nonetheless, occasionally succumb to the effects of sin and idolatry.

The only difference between our old and new natures is that the new nature controls the old nature. As long as we are in this body, sin will still be present in us. So, Humans are idolaters by nature. It is a universal sin of humanity.

We need not picture fetish priests kneeling before stones and woodblocks when we think of idolatry because there are many idolaters today. We don't even need to search afar for idols; all we need to do is stay put and look within; there, we will uncover idols. Idolatry is one sin in our human nature that is most readily committed when we turn away from the living God and create idols of some kind for ourselves. The foundation of idolatry is to love something more than God, to trust something more than God, or to wish we had a different God to the one we have.

It happens when someone has specific enchantments and signs that enable them to recognize God. A person who relies on an external sign or manifestation that may be perceived with the eye or heard with the ear instead of trusting in an invisible God and holding fast to His steadfast promise is practicing idolatry. This major sin, which manifests itself in various ways in every man's heart and even in that of Christians', is the root of a lot of evil.

Satan can easily persuade us to idolize anything, and he does so in a variety of ways. There are many different types of idols, each of which has some inherent value to those who worship them. Although different materials, including wood, stone, metal, and gold, have various values, they are all nonetheless regarded as idols. Depending on their mental capacities and inclinations, people may also make idols out of one material or another.

Many of those idols might be seen as acceptable in and of themselves, but when they are converted into idols, they lose all of their value. God detests all idols, whether they are made of wood or gold. The best and most precious object on earth thus becomes an abomination in God's eyes if we allow it to act as an idol and stand in the way of our relationship with Him. Undoubtedly, many parents idolize their children, many men and women idolize their spouses, and we may even idolize a priest, a president, a supervisor, or a friend. It is also undeniable that many successful businessmen and intelligent men idolize their wealth, success, or even the huge mansions where they live happily.

It makes sense that the ignorant idolize their possessions as gods since they are ignorant and do not know any better. But it is unfortunate when people who have read the Bible more thoroughly and are better versed in its teachings build idols out of anything.

Unfortunately, this is what happens when people rest their faith in simply reading the Bible rather than striving to worship God in a deeply spiritual way. Even the holiest things can become idols in our eyes if they stand in the way of our soul's direct communication with God as He is revealed in Jesus Christ through faith, love, and hope.

> *"A Christian's soul and heart are like a garden where seeds are sowed."*

"*A sower went out to sow seed; and as he sowed, some fell along the traveled path and was trodden underfoot, and the birds of the air ate it up*" (Luke 8:5).

God bought our souls with His own precious blood through the work of Jesus Christ, and through His mercy, He has now entered the scene and taken ownership of them. Our love for everything, including our parents, husband, wife, children, friends, jobs, homes, vehicles, and hobbies, must be expressed in the right context in our hearts and souls. But the King is to be the center of His garden. The heart and soul are not the parent's, the husband's, the wife's, the child's, or the friend's garden. Since our hearts are the King's gardens, we shouldn't depose Jesus Christ as our most beloved King.

Marriage Over Salvation

Another expression, which is as sweet as heaven, is having a loving husband, a contented wife, and a healthy, happy race of children in the home. Many spouses have firmly erected all of their hopes on such a rock and gladly rejected authentic Christianity's beautiful delights. Such husbands and wives believe that marriage, being given in marriage, having children, raising a family, and seeing them all contentedly established are the only permanent things in the world. They are right to treasure and appreciate God's blessings, but it will be out of place for such individuals to make those blessings their exclusive emphasis.

Throughout the book, I have tried to convey a realistic picture of what a mystical, sacred marriage should be for a person. A very lovely and serene image is not the ideal marriage that everyone should aspire to. However, marriage is nothing more than what is modest and proper.

However, if any husband or wife considers marriage the priority over salvation, for which an immortal soul must concentrate its resources, then everything about marriage is inappropriate and everything turns out to be wrong at once.

The Christian can rejoice, and being joyful is not against any law of heaven or earth. Paul explicitly exhorted us to rejoice, and we are free to do so while also fully appreciating God's kindness and the Father who bestowed it upon us. When Paul says that those who have wives should act as though they do not have any, he does not mean to teach us to hate marriage but rather to avoid looking for our heaven in it and letting it get in the way of our serving God.

"I mean, brethren, the appointed time has been winding down and it has grown very short. From now on, let even those who have wives be as if they had none" (1 Corinthians 7:29).

According to popular belief, there are some things that a man without a wife and children can accomplish - things that a man with a wife and children should do. It is believed that a man without a wife can devote his time to serving God; similarly, a man with a wife should do the same. If God has provided him with a wife who will support all of his religious efforts, this will not be difficult for him to do. It is assumed that a man who is single has no worries, but a man who is married should have no worries because God will take care of him and his family. Paul seems to be saying that Christian spouses should keep in mind to hold their spouses, children, and assets with a loose grasp in all of their joys.

We should never place such a high value on our blessings, joys, and marital pleasures that they start to define who we are. Even whether we have a husband, wife, child, property, fortune, or reputation, we should always be prepared to offer everything to God because we know that, in the end, those things are not what matter.

Husbands and wives should act in a manner consistent with having access to springs in heaven that are not prone to drying up during the earth's summer. And that none of the pleasure rivers on earth's surface is larger or deeper than those we have. God wants Christian spouses to stand firm so that nothing on earth can bring us to sorrow or exalt us to the point where we forget God. He wants us to learn to be thankful for all of our material benefits and to take comfort in the fact that our names are recorded in the Lamb's Book of Life.

An Idolized Marriage

God sees humans as the sentient beings that they are - humans. He regards us as such since He has given us free will and the capacity for judgment. God does not apply to the human soul the force that would be acceptable to apply to a piece of metal if it needed to be bored or melted, or even the force that would be acceptable to apply to a piece of wood or animal.

"Be not like the horse or the mule, which lack understanding, which must have their mouths held firm with bit and bridle, or else they will not come with you" (Psalm 32:9).

There is not a single person below heaven whose will God has ever ignored. He has made the Christian's will even freer because of the restrictions that Grace has set on it. Grace liberates the will rather than imprisoning it.

Since Adam and Eve, little has changed in the relationship between a husband and a wife. Given that our skeletons are exactly the same as those of several centuries ago, we appear to be physically identical; and sure enough, the history that was once written about the conduct and crimes of husbands and wives like Ahab and Jezebel, Herod and Herodias, Ananias and Sapphira, etc., may be written again.

"...there is nothing new under the sun" (Ecclesiastes 1:9).

Even if they may be clothed differently, it is the same pair of husbands and wives from long ago. As certain spouses in biblical times upheld their spouses' wishes above God's by murdering God's servants like Naboth and John the Baptist and expelling others like Elijah, there are still couples today who live up to the character of such spouses.

All sins are serious offenses, but some are worse than others. Every sin has the very venom of rebellion and is replete with the vital marrow of betraying God. However, other sins have a more developed version of the fundamental evil of rebellion in them such as abusing, hurting, and hating someone to please a spouse.

Any act of love that draws a person away from Jesus Christ is considered idolatry, and it is terribly worrisome that there are as many idols as there are grains of sand on the beach. Many husbands and wives worship an idol which is known as "pleasing their spouses". They speak and act in a way that will please their spouse while continually hurting God's children and thereby hurting God.

"Any act of love that draws a person away from Jesus Christ is considered idolatry..."

THE THING THEY CALL MARRIAGE

If you have an ordinary tender heart, you will naturally feel the urge to comfort someone when you encounter them in severe sorrow. However, a Christian cannot and should not stand by while another person is suffering without making an effort to help that person.

It would be cruel for a typical Christian to waste time trying to engage people's brains or tickle their fancy when starving people are around us. If they can, they should take more practical action and pay careful attention to the person's immediate needs. If someone is dying of hunger, a Christian ought to feed them. If it's cold, a Christian ought to give them a blanket. A Christian should provide medical attention if there is an illness.

When a situation calls for immediate action, a Christian should stick to the necessities and give their all to what has to be addressed. Any potential misunderstanding between a Christian and a person in need can wait, but what must require our immediate attention.

"But love your enemies and be kind and do good [doing favors so that someone derives benefit from them] and lend, expecting and hoping for nothing in return but considering nothing as lost and despairing of no one." (Luke 6:35).

But suppose Mr. Doe, a devoted Christian, runs into Theodora, who desperately needs comfort. Unfortunately, Mrs. Doe, Mr. Doe's wife, has previously disagreed with Theodora and communicated it with Mr. Doe. Although Mrs. Doe is the guilty party, she won't accept it because she is older and more privileged than Theodora. Yet, Theodora, a godly woman, has taken the initiative to make numerous unsuccessful attempts to finding peace. So, when Mr. Doe encounters Theodora, he interprets her situation as a divine punishment and a chance to exact revenge on behalf of his wife. Mr. Doe may be aware that what he is doing violates God's law, which states:

"You shall not take revenge or bear any grudge against the sons of your people, but you shall love your neighbor as yourself. I am the Lord." (Leviticus 19:18).

He is aware that by turning down Theodora's request for assistance, a nonbeliever will make fun of the Christian God. Theodora may have appealed to Mr. and Mrs. Doe, but her efforts may not have been successful. Even worse, Mrs. Doe might consider her husband's reluctance to help Theodora as a sign of love for her and choose not to weigh in. Mr. and Mrs. Doe may believe they are hurting Theodora, but they may actually be hurting Divine purpose in ways they are oblivious of. Only God can persuade Mr. and Mrs. Doe that hurting another person constitutes a serious offense against God's boundless generosity.

When prompted to take the required action to exalt God and shame the devil, many husbands and wives, like Mr. and Mrs. Doe, have had to say, *Oh, he will actually need aid, but I could not help him.* And when you inquire, *Why couldn't you,* they respond, *I don't want to offend my spouse* or *I needed to get my spouse's permission.*

I do not mean to imply that spouses should intentionally make decisions without consulting each other. That is unacceptable and will only lead to family chaos. I am referring to the fear of one's spouse, the dread of society, and the fear of one's children which keep many people in mental and moral servitude.

Many couples are afraid to act in a way that they know is morally and religiously correct for fear of upsetting their spouses. The greatest of all rights, by which Jesus Christ sets us free, is the freedom to do and accomplish whatever our consciences command in His name. But many couples must ask their spouse to permit them to breathe, think, and feel anything. And nothing makes them more anxious than society. They constantly analyze people's reactions and comments favor their selfishness rather than God's word.

To them, their small community is more important than God whose universe they inhabit. Thousands of lives have been devoured by such an idol of pleasing the spouse and the fear of how they will feel. *What Is Man* is a question that typically runs in the Bible. And it has repeatedly been addressed with a wealth of teaching. David asks God in heaven: *"What is man?" (Psalm 8:4)*.

But I prefer the admonition Isaiah offered the most:

"Cease to trust in [weak, frail, and dying] man, whose breath is in his nostrils [for so short a time]; in what sense can he be counted as having intrinsic worth? (Isaiah 2:22).

"The greatest of all rights, by which Jesus Christ sets us free, is the freedom to do and accomplish whatever our consciences command in His name."

Love Your Neighbor As Yourself

A renowned preacher preached on the sin that Mr. and Mrs. Doe's acts come under. I pray for the ability to communicate very wisely, very passionately, and very honestly as I use it as an illustration. And I pray that any husband and wife who look at Mr. and Mrs. Doe and see themselves in the mirror will be very humble and give in to the reasoning of God's Word.

Humanly speaking, Mr. and Mrs. Doe have no obligation under the law to help Theodora as they currently stand with her. No family law requires them to help her because she is not their biological child. However, a law that renders them responsible for Theodora's needs if they can help her exists in the family of God to which all of them belong. Jesus Christ referred to the expression as the "great commandment".

"...You must love the Lord your God with all your heart and with all your soul and with all your strength and with all your mind; and your neighbor as yourself" (Luke 10:27)

This is due to the fact that the responsibility for us to love our neighbors also falls within the umbrella of the order to love God:

"...You shall love your neighbor as [you do] yourself" (Matthew 22:39).

It is actually contained inside the core of the command to love God since doing so would inevitably lead to loving our neighbor. First, who is it that everyone, including Mr. and Mrs. Doe, is supposed to love? (To love our neighbor as ourselves…). The term "neighbor" refers to a person who is nearby. The word is derived from two archaic words: name or near (near) and buer (to reside); people living or being close by. If anyone is close by, they become our neighbors. The Samaritan felt obligated to love the injured man since he was in his neighborhood and, therefore, neighbor when he spotted him on the road to Jericho. As a result, in the case of Mr. and Mrs. Doe, Theodora is the couple's neigbor because they have seen her and are familiar with her story. Jesus Christ made the commandment:

"And he replied, You must love the Lord your God with all your heart and with all your soul and with all your strength and with all your mind; and your neighbor as yourself" (Luke 10:27)

So how can "You shall love your neighbor as [you do] yoursel" constitute a new commandment? It is in part because the depth of love is fresh. Jesus calls us to love our neighbor as ourselves, but we are also called to love our fellow Christians as much as He loves us - far more than we should love ourselves. Because He loved us so deeply and gave Himself up for us, Jesus Christ loved us better than He loved Himself. Therefore, in the situation involving Mr. and Mrs. Doe and Theodora, "The couple are to love Theodora as a fellow creature, as they both love themselves."

In light of this interpretation of Jesus Christ's instruction, Mr. and Mrs. Doe are to love Theodora, a fellow Christian, in the same way, that Jesus Christ, who died for them, has loved them. In general, that is a higher form of love than the one that every human being should show their neighbors. That is the love of goodness, but this love is one of kinship and intimacy, requiring more self-sacrifice than was mandated by the law of Moses.

Evidently, Mr. and Mrs. Doe value their own well-being; hence, they will not let one another down and will not want to withhold anything pleasant or consoling. Even though they cannot relate to Theodora as they would to themselves, the love of God should compel them to do the same for Theodora if they are willing to obey as Christians.

Sometimes in marriage, a husband and wife's actions become idols not because of what they do but rather because of what they do not do. The sin of doing nothing is one that is not discussed as much as it ought to be. Moses' admonition is obviously directed at the sin of omission:

"But if you will not do so, behold, you have sinned against the Lord; and be sure your sin will find you out." (Numbers 32:23)

If Mr. and Mrs. Doe continue to idolize themselves, disregard God's Word, and refuse to help Theodora, they will inadvertently expose her to all of Satan's temptations, including those of fornication, adultery, apostasy, backsliding, disbelief, etc.

Another way to describe the couple's conduct is un-Christlike, un-brotherhood, and selfish. Theodora needs basic life support, and Mr. and Mrs. Doe, on the other hand, have more than the ordinary person needs. So, what ought to happen to Theodora? They do not seem to care, but it is obvious that if they help Theodora, she can help others, God's church, and the community.

The Doe couple responds:

"Theodora must look to herself. After all, the saying goes: "Each one for himself, and God for us all."

Several couples, notably Mr. and Mrs. Doe, use the phrase,

"And the Lord said to Cain, Where is Abel your brother? And he said, I do not know. Am I my brother's keeper?" (Genesis 4:9).

That young man I know. Years ago, I heard his voice. He goes by the name of Cain, and I want to tell him that while he is not his brother's keeper, he is his brother's murderer. Every human is either their brother or sister's defender or their brother or sister's destroyer. Without a deed or even an intention, a soul murder can be carried out; it frequently happens as a result of negligence. And idolatry in marriage can and has greatly aided in the murder of souls.

Epilogue

Dearly Beloved Reader, I have humbly put before your mind's eye a fair picture of the Solemnity of Singlehood, Marriage, Family, Church, and the State. All of them began as a Home; a word as sweet as heaven, and a healthy, happy race of children is as fine a possession as even angels can desire. However, on the part of God, none of those should be a rock we should build our hopes on; securing as our portion the godly instructions of this book will help us cheerfully renounce the dreamy joys of religion.

God, who dwells in His church, completely frowns on the fact that we regard any of those as the chief end and the real object of our being. If it is in the "WILL" of God, we are to marry and be married.

We should strive to navigate life's difficulties and pleasures with dignity, acquire knowledge, wealth, and comfort, and finally use all the world's privileges without cruelty. We should live a very peaceful and quiet life far distant from the wasteful, immoral, indifferent, or perverted persona that will be an obstacle to others.

"Life is solemn; life is beautiful."

It is equally solemn for all humanity thus far. Life is solemn in the gratitude we owe God for the blessings He is pleased to give us. Life is solemn for work and God's operation. It is true in the solemn humanitarian obligation it imposes on us. Life is solemn to us inasmuch as we can perceive God in it and use it to glorify Him.

The unreality of the solemnity of life to many people in the world is found in the fact that they live for only now. This is the wand that touches the substance and makes it, before the eye of wisdom, dissolve into a shade.

There is another world in view! There is nothing here in the present world but what is proper and right. Yet, everything is improper, and everything becomes wrong at once if they are thought to be the substantial things for which an immortal spirit is to spend its fires and for which an undying soul is to exhaust its powers.

"What is human? And what is marriage, wealth, fame, beauty, etc.? It is not here but gone!" To conclude at once that we come to this world alone, and naked and alone we depart with nothing, we have only to think of what life is when a husband, a wife, and children in a fatal accident are placed in different coffins at their funeral! Such a depiction at funerals is simply a little intermission in the middle of eternity's grandeur, a narrow piece of land sticking out into the great, whether delightful or woeful and unfathomable sea of everlastingness!

Acknowledgment

I am exceedingly grateful to God for making me see much benevolence in action toward me. I gratefully ascribe all glory not to my own effort but to God's grace, mercy, and goodness.

Anyone who knows me well would attest that my life is chock-full of examples of the truth David stated in the following words:

"Your gentleness and condescension have made me…" (Psalm 18:35b).

God's condescension can serve as a comprehensive interpretation of my whole life. It is God's making Himself little, which is the cause of my being able to do anything. I am so little that if God should have manifested His greatness without condescension, I should be trampled under His feet. But God, who must stoop to view the skies and bow to see what angels do, has been gracious to me to bend His eye yet lower and look to the lowly and the contrite and give me grace.

The God who does not sell grace or glory, He who does not put them up to auction to those who can give something in return for them in His robes of grace has been merciful to meet me on the ground of being a nobody and undeserving, and said to me: "I will be gracious unto you." He has given me grace without money, grace without price, and grace without any merit in me. My prayer is to continually love you, God, more than anyone and anything in the world.

Dad, who is now in heaven, you know that I would if I could give everything to maintain an unbroken and intimate fellowship with you. But alas, in this world, our bodies are subject to death, so we do not get or become what we always wish for. While on earth, you were a testimony to what God can do for her daughter through a father. Thank you, Dad, for looking beyond yourself to care for other people's welfare. Love you, Dad! But you do not have the right to be asleep for this long, for your beloved daughter misses you.

To my family: Dads, Moms, Aunts, and Siblings, you know I have a deep love for you for who you all are to me. And I express my appreciation to you all.

For their untold hours of editing and sharing of ideas, I express my heartfelt thanks to Rev. Vincent Davies. You have been a great blessing to me. Without your commitment, this book could not have been completed. To Apostle Retired Joseph Kwame Asabil (Former International Executive Council Member, Church of Pentecost), Agyei Kwarteng (International Executive Council Member, Church Of Pentecost, Area Head Bompata Kumasi), Apostle Michael Kwame Etrue (Executive Council Member, Church of Pentecost, Area Head, Koforidua, and Eastern Region Regional Coordinator), Apostle Samuel Edzii Davidson (Church of Pentecost, Offinso Area Head), Apostle George Kwaku Korankye (Church of Pentecost, United Kingdom), Pastor Kwasi Afoakwah-Duah (Church of Pentecost, Galilea District Accra), and Pastor Richard Nsiah (Church of Pentecost, New York District), Mrs. Faustina Anane-Sarfo, wife of Apostle Isaac Anane-Sarfo, New York Area Head, Church of Pentecost USA INC, I convey my heartfelt gratitude, which words are not able to express, to you. You grabbed the vision and would not let go; despite incredible deadline pressures, you read the necessary material to be able to write an endorsement for the book. Thank you for making God's vision your vision. Whenever I think about what you have done, I envision that day when we all, in a loving fellowship as a church, will come to the great gathering of God, the holy convocation of saints of every tongue, the central home of all the tribes of His great family.

Your collective contribution has well been for solemn purposes; for it is an act for joyous purposes; a solemn joy, a holy delight for the restoration of broken marriages, families, homes, and the world.

I humbly pray that God will forever remember what you have done and bless you accordingly. You have brought me joy.

I am indebted to every priest and wife of the Church of Pentecost and beyond for your godly example.

I humbly thank all ministers and wives of the Church of Pentecost, USA INC. I appreciate their indirect role in gracing every word in the book and providing advice.

I can never stop thinking of the generous advice, consolations, and encouragement that some women and men in my life rendered to me when I needed it most. You have prayed with me to advance this worthy cause. There is wisdom in many counselors. Your love, prayers, and advice are invaluable.

I am grateful to all of you who have shared your personal experiences regarding Singleness, Marriage, Family, etc. Your testimonies will not only inspire others, but they will also make this book more appealing.

They provide not only informative examples but also spectacular key points along the journey. It's mesmerizing! Thank you very much.

As I put down my pen for the last time, I humbly offer a blessing to everyone who reads this book. May the grace of our Lord Jesus Christ and the Son of God be with you. May the grace of that exceptional Person who is God and Man in one Person and who is the church's bridegroom continue to be solemnly bestowed on you. May the grace that comes with His supremacy, His kingship, and His divinely human sovereignty come to you all.

Holy Spirit, I will be forever grateful to You.

WELCOME TO OUR PARACLETE FAMILY!!

Whether you received this book as a gift, borrowed it, or purchased it yourself, we are glad you read it. It is just one of the many helpful, insightful, and encouraging resources produced by our Paraclete family.

Many Christians have long been Christians, have grown rich in experience, and known God's love and faithfulness.

Please, let us look out for the little ones, and speak to them goodly and in comfortable words, whereby they may be cheered and strengthened. When we determine the little ones have weakness, in the plentitude of our wisdom and experience, we need to advice and train them. Let's not withhold graces from them when we have no intention to help them get better and become useful to the family of God and the communities of the world.

Please, let's act in a noble and a virtuous part to cheer the little ones up and bade them of good courage. Some have been wounded not because of their faults but by the people they trusted. Therefore, let's please salute them with words of tender encouragement; for this is precisely what Christians do.

Above all else, let's cease not to pray for the little ones till their little heart is completely and forever given to God. Be a Prophet Samuel to the little ones as he was to David. Be a Naomi to the little ones, and she was to Ruth. Be an Elizabeth to the little ones as she was to Mary, for you may be nurturing a king of Israel or a descendant of Jesus Christ, the Savior of the world.

In fact, that is what the Paraclete is all about - providing inspiration, comfort, advocacy, guidance, information, and godly advice to people in all stages of life.

May our Paraclete, the Third Person of the Blessed Trinity, enlighten us so that we will know that we are one family fighting a common enemy called Satan. May He bless us so that we can be a blessing to everyone that comes our way. Amen!

EMAIL US YOUR STORY!!!

Please, give us the privilege of hearing how the conversations in AS IT WAS IN THE BEGINNING have impacted you, your Single Life, your Marriage, your Family or your Loved One.

Email Ewuramma via:
ourparacletefoundation.inc@gmail.com

Our Paraclete Foundation Inc. is a non-profit organization established to bring to remembrance that everyone is the DARLING of God.

Our objective is to let every person know and feel that God loves us unconditionally so that as a natural result, we will love Him in return; and in proportion, as our love knowledge increases, our faith strengthens, and our conviction to love one another deepens, the world will know that we are really ONE FAMILY AND FROM ONE RACE.

I pray that God will grant us the grace so that the very constitution of our being will be constrained to yield our hearts to God into building godly human and marriage relationships.

Appendix

1. City upon a Hill - Wikipedia. https://en.wikipedia.org/wiki/City_upon_a_Hill

2. Dedham Pulpit: Or, Sermons by the Pastors of the First Church in Dedham in ... - Ebenezer Burgess, First Church (Dedham, Mass.) - Google Llibres. https://books.google.ad/books?pg=PA343&vq=%22O+ye+hypocrites,+ye+can+discern+the+face+of+the+sky,+but+can+ye+not+discern+the+signs+of+the%22&dq=editions:OXFORD590230206&lr=&id=hDoPAAAAIAAJ&hl=ca&output=text

3. Finishing | Jesus Speaks. https://jesusspeaks.com/tag/finishing/

4. Potential secretary of state Mitt Romney met Donald Trump at Jean Georges in Trump Tower and ate chocolate cake with Reince Priebus. https://qz.com/849010/potential-secretary-of-state-mitt-romney-met-donald-trump-at-jean-georges-in-trump-tower-and-ate-chocolate-cake-with-reince-priebus

5. Purity & Chastity Â–Heir Force Ministries. href="https://goheirforce.com/library/devotionals/daily-reading-plan/sacrifices-in-the-temple/purity-chastity/">https://goheirforce.com/library/devotionals/daily-reading-plan/sacrifices-in-the-temple/purity-chastity/

6. The Encapsulation Of Seed Technology (Part 2): The Expedition To The Holy Estate | INFEMI Sermon By Minister Evans Ochieng, Ân Infinite Fellowship Ministries. https://

Appendix

infemi.org/2019/09/22/the-encapsulation-of-seed-technology-part-2-the-expedition-to-the-holy-estate-infemi-sermon-by-minister-evans-ochieng/

7. The election of Barack Obama. https://theologicalpipe.com/2008/11/08/the-election-of-barack-obama/

8. Trouble on the Hill | thinkinthemorning.com. https://thinkinthemorning.com/trouble-on-the-hill/

9. Why The Russia Investigation Matters And Why You Should Care. https://www.spokanepublicradio.org/2017-05-24/why-the-russia-investigation-matters-and-why-you-should-care

10. じじぃの「歴史・思想_403_2050 年 世界人口大減少・最強のアメリカ」 - cool-hiraÂ's diary. < href="https://cool-hira.hatenablog.com/entry/2020/12/18/060810">https://cool-hira.hatenablog.com/entry/2020/12/18/060810

END OF VOLUME ONE

www.ingramcontent.com/pod-product-compliance
Lightning Source LLC
Chambersburg PA
CBHW071901290426
44110CB00013B/1239